A Theology of Ministry

Michael G. Lawler

Sheed & Ward

Sheed & Ward™ is a service of National Catholic Reporter Publishing Company, Inc.

Library of Congress Catalog Card Number: 89-61929

ISBN: 1-55612-310-8

Published by: Sheed & Ward
115 E. Armour Blvd., P.O. Box 419492
Kansas City, MO 64141-6492

To order, call: (800) 333-7373

Contents

This one's for David

Introduction

I know exactly when I became *really* interested in ministry in the church. It was in September, 1962. I was then a student in Rome, entertaining an English friend and his sister visiting Rome for the first time. Since both are now well-known, each for a different reason, I owe them anonymity, and so I shall call him Charles and her Priscilla. Charles had come to Rome after being ordained an Anglican priest earlier in the summer; Priscilla had come along, at least we two males thought, just for the ride.

The itinerary for their first full day in Rome called for the Circus Maximus, the Forum and the Capitoline Hill. I could not be in that part of Rome without visiting one of the locals' favorite spots, *La Bocca della Verità,* the Mouth of Truth. Roman parents keep their children honest by telling them its legend: if you put your hand in *La Bocca* and then lie, it will bite off your hand. Charles put in his hand and said: "I am a priest of the Catholic church." When nothing happened, I thought to myself, so much for legends. Priscilla then put in her hand and said solemnly: "Some day I, too, will be a priest of the Catholic church." Still The Mouth did nothing—though Charles guffawed and I, more politely, smiled benignly at her joke.

That night, as we ate spaghetti carbonara just off the Via della Conciliazione, the three of us discussed our reactions to both statements. Young and fiercely apologetic Roman Catholic as I then was (I am now an older, wiser Roman Catholic), I pointed out to Charles Leo XIII's judgment on his ordination, "absolutely null and utterly void." Though I had some hesitations about the argument of *Apostolicae Curae,* and particularly about the political maneuvering that preceded it, in 1962 I was in no position to take theological issue with what I took to be a solemn papal judgment. When the discussion turned to Priscilla's statement, I left to

Charles the task of explaining the undeniable fact that priesthood was a male profession, always had been, always would be.

Priscilla was not easily convinced. I had the impression that she had had this discussion before and was better primed for it than the Anglican priest or the budding Roman Catholic theologian. Her arguments rested on the human equality of men and women, *'adam*, before God, an equality reaffirmed and renewed by Christian initiation. I noticed that, while her arguments were both anthropologically and theologically restrained, Charles' tended to be lofty and authoritarian. What was at stake, he pointed out, had nothing to do with anthropology but with the long catholic tradition of being faithful to the explicit desires of Jesus.

Since, however, she was his sister, I left the field to them. I kept to myself the trenchant thought that if the ordination of Anglican men was "absolutely null and utterly void," how much more absolutely and utterly void would be the ordination of Anglican women. For the not-too-skilled Roman theologian, both questions were in the same category: *Closed*.

Their last day in Rome was a momentous day in the history of the Roman Catholic Church, for it coincided with the opening of the Second Vatican Council. Charles gloried in the high-church pageantry and commented that, if the outcome of the Council was half as impressive as its beginning, things would never be the same in the Roman Catholic Church. I had never seen him in the role of prophet, but with hindsight I now know that his statement was undeniably true. That very first day of the Council produced drama, the rejection of the prepared document on revelation. The drama was repeated in November, when the prepared document on the church was even more resoundingly rejected. The *aggiornamento* that Pope John XXIII had called for in his opening speech, though most of us did not yet realize it, was under way.

On a damp Roman night that November, when the furor over the rejection of the document on the church was still at its height, I attended a lecture by a French Dominican priest. His name, quite unknown then not only to me but also to most in attendance, was Yves-Marie Congar. His topic, not surprisingly given what we know of him now, was "The

Church." His lecture proved to be one of those moments in life that appear innocuous at the time but, on reflection, turn out to be seminal and trans-formational. After Congar and Vatican II, and the two are not entirely separable when the talk is of church, Catholic visions of church would never be the same.

Congar said three things that night that have stayed with me and have moved me since. He said that the church can never be adequately dealt with as a perfect society available for quasi-scientific analysis, but that it is rather a mystery available only for communal and personal faith. He said that both the theory and the practice of ministry reflect an underlying theory of church and that, therefore, if we change our vision of church, we change also our vision of ministry. He said, finally, that women and men are equal in the eyes of God and that, therefore, they should be equal in the eyes of God's church and should be drawn more equitably into the minis-try of the church. We shall see that those themes made their various ways into the Dogmatic Constitution on the Church which the Council approved finally on November 21, 1964.

The actors in those 1962 dramas have, of course, all grown up, and *La Bocca della Verità* has been vindicated. Charles is not only a priest of the Catholic church, but now also a bishop; Priscilla is now the priest she said she would be. Yves-Marie Congar is now eighty-four years of age, bedrid-den for the past four years, but still at work on the building up of the church. His latest book, *Entretiens d'automne* (Cerf, 1987), is very critical of the fear of modernity and renewedness that many of the Catholic hierar-chy bring to the legacy of the Council. After many years of reflection on the ecclesial themes of that Council and after many years of practicing ministry, alone and with others, I join him in that faithful criticism in this book about ministry in the ministerial church.

I see this book as a much-needed contribution to the discussion of min-istry in the church, especially in the contemporary world where Christians of all denominations continue to misunderstand their universal call to min-istry on behalf of the kingdom of God. I see it as bringing to conscious-ness the invitation issued by Jesus and recently explained by John Paul II as being issued to *all* Christ's faithful: "You go into the vineyard too"

(Matt. 20:4).[1] I see it as patterned after the suggestions first received from Congar twenty-seven years ago, and therefore after *Lumen Gentium,* the Dogmatic Constitution on the Church, itself patterned after those suggestions.

The book deals first with a vision of church, on which a vision of ministry is essentially dependent (Chapter One). It then deals with ministry in the church, offering and explaining its definition (Chapter Two). It proceeds to confront the question of priesthood in the church, first the common ecclesial priesthood of every believer and then the ordained priesthood of the church's leaders (Chapter Three). There follows a treatment of laity in the church (Chapter Four) and ordained priesthood (Chapter Five). These two chapters seek to differentiate the respective roles of lay persons and of priests in the ministry of the church, while maintaining that their differentiation is always to be understood as secondary to their original unity as the People of God and the Body of Christ. Finally, because I believe that it is now past time for the church to acknowledge and accept the Spirit's gifts in its female members, Priscilla's and Junia's sisters in faith, and to stimulate in its every member, female and male alike, a sense of communion and responsibility, there is a detailed treatment of women in ministry (Chapter Six).

There are many who have already told me, and I presume many more who will tell me, that these are dangerous times for theologians. I confess, however, I am still impressed by the freedom I enjoy as a Catholic theologian. I accept without fear the teaching of the Second Vatican Council. "All the faithful, clerical and lay, possess a lawful freedom of inquiry and thought, and the freedom to express their minds humbly about those matters in which they enjoy competence."[2]

I admit that the freedom of inquiry I possess in the church is not an unlimited freedom, but one that is bound to both truth and ecclesial responsibility. I understand that it is not for theologians to formulate either the doctrine or the practice of their church; that task is for others. The theologian's task is one "of interpreting the documents of the past and present magisterium, of putting them in the context of the whole of revealed truth, and of finding a better understanding of them by the use of hermeneutics." That is a task which embraces a risky critical function, which I acknowledge should "be exercised positively rather than destructively."[3] It is as such a critical and constructive interpretation that I offer this work.

There is an important item that must be introduced here, and finished with here, so that it does not constantly intrude into both the process and the content of this book. It is an ancient epistemological item, namely, human language, human knowledge and the essential nature of God. As women in the Christian churches try to translate their vision of equal discipleship into equal gender-language, its contemporary incarnation takes place in the discussion of the gender pronouns to be applied to God, he or she, him or her. I have no universally acceptable solution to the legitimately vexing question of God-talk. My approach to it, however, at least situates it in the two universal traditions which have shaped the catholic tradition.

The first of these traditions is the biblical tradition, whose revelation on the question of God-talk is articulated most trenchantly by the Book of Deuteronomy. "Since you saw no form on the day that the Lord spoke to you at Horeb out of the midst of the fire, beware lest you act corruptly by making a graven image for yourselves, in the form of any figure, in the *likeness of male or female*" (4:15-16). The second is the theological tradition which, in its own way, underscored the biblical suspicion of images of God. Thomas Aquinas is an ancient spokesman for that tradition. "Anything about God is entirely unknown to men and women in this life, that is, it is unknown what God *is*."[4] John Paul II is a contemporary spokesman for the same tradition.[5]

Questions about human life, its beginning and its end, its meaning, what lies beyond it, abound in human history. If there is a beyond, it is beyond human experience and its limited capacity to deal precisely only with sensible reality. It is a beyond, therefore, that is dealt with only in images, for what lies beyond sensible reality is dealt with only in images. It is a Beyond that in the Jewish and the Christian traditions is named *God* who, even after revelation, "dwells in unapproachable light" and "whom no man has ever seen or can see" (1 Tim. 6:16).

Is the religious and theological language the way it is with God? Are the images of God as person and trinity and creator and father and love really photographs of the way God actually *is*? There are two answers to those questions. The first, and preliminary, answer is yes; that is the way God is in the Christian tradition. The second, and definitive, answer is no; that is not the way God ultimately *is*. The language is not photograph or transcript but image and analogy, which enable men and women to model, understand, relate to and experience God. It is, as Aquinas says, not the way God *is*.

Despite the universal tradition, Meister Eckhart still had to chide medieval theologians and believers about their God-talk and about their literal understanding of it. "Why do you prate of God? Whatever you say of him is untrue." Von Balthasar feels obliged to continue to chide their contemporary counterparts.[6] Whatever women and men say of God is untrue ultimately, for it is only image and analogy to enable understanding. It does not reveal what God *is*, but only what God *is like* and simultaneously *not like*. God is like a person but not exactly like a human person, like a creator but not exactly like a human creator, like a father but not exactly like a human father, like a mother but not exactly like a human mother. God is, indeed, most like *'adam,* man and woman together (Gen. 5:2), for they together are made in God's likeness (Gen. 1:26).[7]

Man and woman are both made in God's likeness. Both *he/him* and *she/her* are equal likenesses of God, though human gender pronouns are not ultimately what God is like. For, however much woman and man are like God and however much God is, therefore, like them, neither man nor woman is ultimately the exact replica of God. They each offer metaphorical and analogical likeness to promote insight and understanding but, even after the insight they promote, God remains what God *is* for them, ultimate Mystery.

Since neither *he* nor *she,* therefore, is the way God ultimately is; since both *he* and *she* offer truth about God only as image and analogy provoking insight and understanding; since both *he* and *she* offer untruth when they are taken to be the way God ultimately *is*; throughout this book, I shall use them both of God. I shall use the male pronouns in chapters one, three and five, and the female ones in chapters two, four and six. I do not pretend that this is the ultimate solution to the problem of inclusive language. I employ it in this book only to underscore Aquinas' injunction: neither *he* nor *she* can tell me or anyone else precisely what God essentially *is*. This book is constructed on the simple premise that, for us men and women, God and all that is connected with her are ultimately Mystery.[8]

No author writes a book without influence from others, and I am delighted to confess that I am no exception to that rule. I freely acknowledge the influence of past teachers and the provocation of countless students, past and present, who pushed me to theological consistency in my ecclesiology and ministeriology. Since I cannot name them all, I will not name any. That way any error will be obviously and exclusively mine. I name only my son, David, from whom I have learned empathy with others and to whom this book is dedicated. It seems to me, at least, propitious that this book was finished on that ancient feast of the manifestation of God called Epiphany.

Michael G. Lawler
Creighton University

1.

Called To Be Church

The Second Vatican Council and the Church

Yves Congar, the greatest ecclesiologist of this or any other century, has always insisted that a theology of ministry reflects an underlying theology of church. If this is true, and I believe that it demonstrably is, any search for a theology of ministry must begin with a theology of church.

Throughout the past twenty years many claimants have been put forward for the title of the most fundamental document of the Second Vatican Council. Such claims are usually advanced more to support whatever a speaker or writer has to say than to offer an objective, theological assessment. I hope I am not engaging in similar theological bias when I say that the only such claim that is valid is the claim made on behalf of *Lumen Gentium*, the Dogmatic Constitution on the Church.

I make this claim because all other documents can be shown to be derived from this one and to be dependent upon it. The Second Vatican Council was ultimately a Council *of* the church, *for* the church and *about* the church. The Extraordinary Synod of 1985 was utterly correct in insisting that the most important teaching of the Council was the vision it presented of the church as a *koinonia,* communion, a fact which John Paul II confirmed in his Apostolic Exhortation on the Laity.[9] A brief chronology of the Constitution's journey to approval will both highlight its conceptual renewedness in the Catholic theological tradition, and provide us with an underlying ecclesiology to support a contemporary theology of ministry.

1

By the time the preparatory document *De Ecclesia,* authored by the Central Theological Commission, was distributed to the Council Fathers in November, 1962, the direction of the Second Vatican Council had already been dramatically established. In his opening address to the Council, his famous *aggiornamento* speech, Pope John XXIII had asked the Council to formulate Catholic doctrine in language appropriate to the times. A few days before they received *De Ecclesia,* the Fathers had discussed and rejected the document on *The Sources of Revelation,* largely on the basis that it made no effort to articulate Catholic doctrine on revelation in contemporary language. After the drama of the rejection of the Central Theological Commission's document on revelation, it came as no surprise to anyone that its submission on the church met with the same fate. It was sent back to the Commission with the instructions that it should be, not just touched up cosmetically, but reworked radically to bring it into line with the terms of Pope John's instructions.

When the reformed sub-commission met to reconsider *De Ecclesia* in February, 1963, fifteen new schemas and hundreds of suggestions for improvement had been submitted to it. Many of them agreed on a common, four-chapter structure for the document, the chapters dealing respectively with the nature of the church, hierarchy in the church, especially the episcopate, laity in the church and the ecclesiological significance of the states of perfection in the church. There was also a strong movement to include a proposed schema on the Blessed Virgin as a chapter in the document.

The changes that were incorporated into this four-chapter schema before it was finally approved and forwarded to the Council for discussion in September, 1963, were already indications of a contemporary Roman Catholic theology of church. The chapter on the *nature* of the church gave way to one on the *mystery* of the church; the chapter on the *laity* gave way to a much-expanded one on the *People of God,* including the laity; and the narrow, traditional chapter on the *states of perfection* in the church gave way to a more expansive one on the call of all in the church to holiness. The stage was set for a dramatically renewed vision of church in the Roman Catholic tradition.

When it came to the floor of the Council for discussion in October, 1963, the new document received generally positive approbation, particularly for its efforts to present the church in biblical terms and to focus on some doctrinal aspects that had long been obscured, the theology of the laity, for instance, and the sacramentality of the episcopate. But there was still some opposition. The document, some thought, still presented the church in terms that were too static and triumphalist, ignoring its dynamic, historical dimension and the eschatological transformation it awaited. Its proof-texting approach to scripture, that is, its citing of texts to prove a doctrine assumed to be true rather than seeking to uncover genuine Christian teaching from unbiased exegesis of the scriptural record, was also challenged. But all in all, the document was judged to be an acceptable basis for discussion, and on October 1, 1963, the vote reflected that approval (2231 placet, 43 non-placet, 27 illegible votes).

From the discussion on Chapter One, now "The *Mystery* of the Church" rather than "The *Nature* of the Church," there emerged a widespread demand for a greater elaboration of the biblical images of church, especially those that highlighted its dynamic, historical and eschatological aspects rather than its institutional character. The discussion on Chapter Two, which sought to establish dogmatically and precisely the office and role of episcopacy in the church, proved to be lively, long-drawn out and very, very tense. The first Vatican Council had proposed to deal with this question in 1870, but had been brought to a premature close by the advancing armies of Victor Emmanuel and the outbreak of the Franco-Prussian War. When the question surfaced again, almost one hundred years later, its discussion kept bumping against two things: the one-sided teaching of Vatican I about the position of the Roman Pontiff in the church, and the development of that teaching in the post-conciliar theological tradition.

The discussion on Chapter Three was uneventful, though there was an insistent demand that it be divided into two sections, the first dealing with the People of God and the other with the laity. Chapter Four was doomed before discussion of it ever started, for there was widespread agreement that it was too narrowly conceived and too hurriedly put together just to replace the previous schema. There emerged a demand for it, too, to be split into two chapters, one dealing with the call of all in the church to holiness and the other dealing specifically with that call as lived by vowed religious. Though it did not win final approval in the Second Session, the movement to include a chapter on the Blessed Virgin gathered enough support to ensure that it would be added later.

By the end of the Second Session in the Fall of 1963, then, an entirely new schema on the church had taken shape. It was more theological in concept, more communal and dynamic in approach and much more contemporary in language than the original document *De Ecclesia*. It had eight chapters, suggestively arranged: 1) The Mystery of the Church; 2) The People of God; 3) The Hierarchical Structure of the Church; 4) The Laity; 5) The Call of the Whole Church to Holiness; 6) Religious; 7) The Eschatological Nature of the Pilgrim Church; 8) The Role of the Blessed Virgin Mary, the Mother of God, in the Mystery of Christ and the Church. The Dogmatic Constitution on the Church, *Lumen Gentium,* which was approved by the Council during its Third Session on November 21, 1964 (2151 placet, 5 non-placet), was essentially the document that emerged from the Second Session.

The Dogmatic Constitution on the Church

Lumen Gentium is the *Magna Carta* for any subsequent theological discussion of church in the Roman Catholic tradition. It did not say all there is to say about church. In fact, its decision to initiate its discussion with the insistence that the church is *mystery* was intended to proclaim openly that the last word about a pilgrim church is never possible until its pilgrimage reaches its end.

Pope Paul VI had emphasized this very point in his opening address to the Second Session. "The church is a mystery," he said, "that is, a reality impregnated with the presence of God and, therefore, of such a nature that there are ever-new and deeper explorations of it possible."[10] Pope John Paul II reaffirmed it at the closing of the Synod on the Laity in the Fall of 1987. The church "is a great mystery," he said, "and how do we communicate mystery?"[11] The Council's insistence on discussing the church under the heading *mystery* rather than under the original heading *nature* was meant to direct attention to the divine innerness of the church rather than to its external structure. Before it is an external institution, the church is a mystery, a reality in the human world which at one and the same time both reveals and conceals the presence of God.

During his pilgrimage to the Holy Land in 1964, Pope Paul VI called for a successful conclusion to the Council. "We must assure the church," he said, "a new way of thinking, of willing, of acting." The Constitution on the Church gave him what he wanted, a new way of thinking about church, of speaking about church, of willing and of acting as church. It provided a vision of what church was in its inner reality rather than what it was in its external structure.

Schillebeeckx describes the ecclesiology of the Constitution in this way. There is a vertical decentralization from church to Christ. There is also a threefold horizontal decentralization: from Roman primacy to universal episcopacy, from hierarchical ministry to the People of God, from the Roman Catholic church to other Christian churches.[12]

The transition from the preparatory document to the one that was finally approved was a transition from a conception of church that was institutional and structural to one that underscored communion, mystery and grace. It was a transition from a fixation on ecclesiastical office and obedience to law to a fascination with personal charism and co-responsibility. It was a transition from a focus on Roman primacy to a focus on ecclesial collegiality. It was a transition from what Christians see when they look at the church from the outside to what they believe the church to be in its internal reality. The suggestive rearrangement of the four chapters of the second document into the final eight, and especially the emphasis intended by placing chapters on the mystery of the church and on the People of God before one on the hierarchy, gave ample evidence of the Fathers' conviction that the church is a community of believers before it is a hierarchical institution.

Lumen Gentium affirmed that the church *is* mystery, *is* a communion of faith, hope and love, *is* a pilgrim people, *is* sacrament of Christ in the world, long before it *has* external forms and hierarchical structures. It speaks at length, and rightly so, of those forms and structures. But it speaks of them only as the external forms of what really counts, namely a people of faith and hope and love called into, and sustained in being, by God and on its pilgrim way to him. However *renewed* this vision of church might be for twentieth century Christians, since it recovers ancient ecclesiological themes from the Fathers of the church, it can hardly be considered a *new* vision. Old or new, we need to consider it at some length.

Church as Theocentric, Christocentric and Pneumatocentric

The vertical decentralization that Schillebeeckx notes is exactly correct. The church is Christocentric. It exists only since Christ, only in Christ, only for Christ and for the God he reveals. Christ is the alpha and the omega of church: who he was, what he said, what he did and, above all, who and how he continues to be for us here and now. In his monumental *Jesus,* Schillebeeckx was moved to put it uncharacteristically simply. "The heart of Christianity is not just the abiding message of Jesus and its definitive relevance, but the persisting eschatological relevance of his person."[13]

Jesus the Christ himself, not just his memory or his message, is at the heart of the church. Therein lies, at least in part, the mystery of the church, for how can a person ever be caught definitively in human statements, however orthodox they might be. If it is ever separated from him, absolutized in itself, considered only in its external, historical aspects, the church ceases to be holy mystery and becomes just one more human institution among the many in the world. The church is not only an institution which Christ established; it is also, and mysteriously, a communion of men and women who are incorporated into Christ and who all share in Christ's life.[14] It is a community which now embodies Christ in the present world, as surely as the humanity provided by Mary once embodied him in the past. It is, as the tradition has consistently insisted that it is, his very Body.

The Council insists several times on this Christ-centered character of the church. "Christ is the light of the nations," it proclaims, not the church.[15] Any light that is in the church is but a reflection of the light of Christ. Christ is the sun and the church but a moon reflecting the sun's light to the world,[15] by proclaiming the gospel to every creature (cf. Mark 16:15).

"Christ is always present in his church, especially in her liturgical celebrations." He is present in her celebration of eucharist, both in the eucharistic species and in her ministers. He is present in her sacraments by his power, "so that when a man baptizes it is really Christ himself who baptizes."[17] He is present in his word, for it is he who speaks when it is proclaimed. He is present when the church gathers to pray, "for he promised: 'Where two or three are gathered together for my sake, there am I in the midst of them' (Matt. 18:20)."[18] Christ is at the heart of everything that the church does as church. The essential being of the church is, therefore, easily summed up. It is being-faithful, to Christ and to his summons to be his Body.

If the church cannot be conceived without reference to Christ, neither can it be conceived without reference to the Counselor-Spirit whom he promised to send (John 14:16,26). It is only because, and to the extent that, it is rooted in Christ and his Spirit that the church can produce the good fruit of life with God. If the Old Testament can be described as the revelation of God, the New Testament as the revelation of the Son who makes the Father known, the church can be described as the revelation of the Holy Spirit, who reveals the trinitarian nature of God and makes it possible for all to share that trinitarian life.

The Council proclaims that "when the work which the Father had given the Son to do on earth was accomplished, the Holy Spirit was sent on the day of Pentecost in order that he might forever sanctify the church, and thus all believers would have access to the Father through Christ in the one Spirit."[19] The Spirit of Christ and of the church is always a creative Spirit, fashioning believers into the one Body of Christ, anointing this Body and making it mysteriously *Christos,* Christ.[20] The Spirit also distributes gifts, charismata, among "the faithful of every rank" to make then fit for the varied tasks which are to be done for the building up of the Body.[21]

Charismata, which the Spirit continues to distribute abundantly today, are "given to everyone for profit" (1 Cor.12,7). But that profit is not for the individual to whom the gift is given. Charism is never for personal power or glory. It is always for the edification or the building up of the church (cf. Eph.4:12). It comes down vertically from the Spirit of God to be shared horizontally with every member of the church.

If the church is centered on Christ and on his Spirit, it is necessarily centered also on the Father-Mother God who sends them both. This God sent his "Son into the world, not to condemn the world, but that the world might be saved by him" (John 3:17 and passim). He was well-pleased with this Son (Mark 1:11; Matt.3:17), so well-pleased indeed that he raised him from the dead and made him manifest to Peter and to the other apostles (1 Cor 15:4; Acts 2:24). His resurrection of Jesus and his making him manifest, as we shall see, was the initial summons which called the church into existence. There would have been no Christian church, because there would have been no Christ, without this benevolent God. Nor would there have been available to the church without him the myriad charisms of the Spirit, including *the* gift, the Spirit himself. For he it is who sends this other Counselor to teach all things and to bring to memory all that Jesus said and did (John 14:26).

Everything that makes church and on which church depends is from the God who wishes men and women "to be saved and to come to the knowledge of the truth" (1 Tim.2:4). It is because he has gathered together as church all those who look upon Jesus as savior that the church is the community of salvation, the very sacrament of salvation in the world. The church relies on God the Father for its very existence, and it is only to the degree that it acknowledges and acts upon this radical theocentric character that it can claim to be church at all.

The christocentric, pneumatocentric and theocentric dimensions of the church give ecclesiology a different focus from the overly triumphalist attitudes of recent centuries. The Constitution declares that the primordial elements in the church are the mysterious and sanctifying presences of the Father-Mother God, of his Christ and of his Spirit, not structures or laws or rituals or institutions. If the church is to be faithful to the Christ and to the God he reveals, and thus survive the gates of hell, it will not be because of good organization or infallible doctrine. It will be because of the indefectible presence and saving action of the trinitarian God.

A brief glance at the manuals *De Ecclesia* written between the Council of Trent and the Second Vatican Council will reveal what scant attention they paid to the presence of God in the church. Though they did not go quite as far as the third-century Syrian Document, *Didascalia Apostolorum,* which presents the Bishop as occupying the place of the Father, the Deacon as occupying the place of the Son and the Presbyter as occupying the place of a simple apostle,[22] they did give inordinate attention to organization and structure. The great novelty of the Constitution on the Church is that it returns any consideration of church to the mysterious presence of God within it and asserts that this presence, not any external structure or organization, constitutes its very essence as a community of salvation.

Church as Sacrament

Because the saving work of God in Christ continues to be mysteriously efficacious in it, the church "is a kind of sacrament or sign of intimate union with God, and of the unity of all mankind."[23] "God has gathered together as one all those who in faith look upon Jesus as the author of salvation and the source of unity and peace, and has established them as church, that for each and for all she may be the visible sacrament of this saving unity."[24]

The sacramental character of the church follows directly from its Christocentric and Pneumatocentric dimensions. To say that the church is sacrament is to say that it is "a symbol of a sacred reality, a visible form of invisible grace."[25] It is to say that it is both a sign of union with God and an instrument which God uses to achieve this union. Grace, which is a theological code word for God,[26] and sacrament, which is a theological code word for symbol, belong together in the human world. The invisible God or Grace needs visible form to be embodied in the world, and sacraments of all kinds provide a variety of forms. Sacraments, that is, are points of intersection between the human and the divine. God, who dwells in inaccessible mystery, first makes sacraments necessary in the human world and then sacraments make God or Grace explicitly present.[27]

As sacrament of the God who "desires all men to be saved and to come to the knowledge of the truth" (1 Tim. 2:4), the church is a point of intersection between this invisible God and visible men and women. At this point, the mysterious God is rendered explicitly present to and for all. Faith and sacrament are indispensable cornerstones of the church; faith in the God who wishes to save all as he saved the church; faith in the sacramental church and in its task of making this God explicitly present. Where faith in this God is absent, to that extent church is absent; where church fails to be adequate sacrament of this God, to that extent also it fails to be church.

Prior to any functional differentiations in the church is a mysterious unity of all its members in and with the trinitarian God. It is "a people made one with the unity of the Father, the Son and the Holy Spirit."[28] The great sacraments of Christian initiation create this unity in the Body of Christ (baptism), celebrate and confer the charism to bear witness to the Body and to the Christ (confirmation), and proclaim, make explicit and celebrate an ever more intense incorporation into this Body and this Christ (eucharist). All the members of the Body, whoever they are, are called to and have, therefore, a right to "expend all their energy in the growth of the church and its continuous sanctification."[29] The life of mystery-grace, which is at the heart of the church, is decisive in its constitution. Every member without exception, lay or clerical, is called to, has the duty to and, therefore, the right to, proclaim this grace for the building up of the church and for the salvation of the world.

With this category of sacramental unity in and with the trinitarian God, the Second Vatican Council sought to restore an equilibrium which had been upset over the years. After the First Vatican Council in 1870, a Council which, we must never forget, had not yet reached mid-stream before it was unceremoniously ended by the outbreak of war, the church isolated the Bishop of Rome as the visible root, trunk and branch of authority in the church. Though fundamentally correct, this position was overly exaggerated. Vatican Council II sought to right the imbalance it created by emphasizing the idea of *collegiality.*

When the public press, which can be forgiven for not knowing any better, and some of the Catholic press which is not so easily excused, speak of collegiality, they often intend only the collegiality of all the bishops with the Bishop of Rome. In the same vein, when they speak of *concelebration* they usually intend only a number of priests celebrating eucharist together. But as the ancient meaning of concelebration intended the whole community, and not merely its *sacerdos,* offering the bread and the wine,[30] so also the modern meaning of collegiality intends the whole community, and not just its bishops, sharing responsibility for the church. The church of Christ is truly present, the Constitution on the Church teaches, "in all legitimate local congregations of the faithful which, united with their pastors, are themselves called churches in the New Testament. For in their own locality these are the new people called by God."[31]

Karl Rahner had this notion of truly ecclesial collegiality in mind when he wrote that "the most humble, the most loving, the most holy, the most apparently obscure person in the church, and not the Pope, is at the top of the hierarchy, the real hierarchy for which the church is only a means."[32] His statement is but an echo of a text from the Constitution on the Church, so glowingly praised by Paul VI in his homily to a Congress of Lay Apostolate.[33] "The laity are gathered together in the People of God and make up the Body of Christ under one Head. Whoever they are, they are called upon, as living members, to expend all their energy for the growth of the church and its continuous sanctification. . . . Upon all the laity, therefore, rests the noble duty of working to extend the divine plan of salvation ever increasingly to all men of each epoch and in every land."[34] The realization of how far we still are from appreciating that ideal twenty five years after the approval of the Constitution is sobering.

Church as Eschatological

In 1943, in his encyclical *Mystici Corporis,* which followed the theological lines laid down in Tromp's *Corpus Christi Quod Est Ec-clesia,*[35] Pius XII declared that the Body of Christ is identified exclusively with the Roman Catholic Church. The preparatory document offered to the Council this same identification between the Body of Christ and the Roman Catholic Church. It was an identification which the Council deplored[37] and, after intense debate, rejected. The Body of Christ, it taught, is not identical with the Roman Catholic Church, but "subsists in the Catholic Church."[37] The Catholic Church is part of the Body of Christ, but far from all of it, in the same way that the United States is part of America but far from all of it. Christ and Catholic, Catholic and Christian, are not to be thought of as identical, for all the Christian churches await a final transformation in which God will be all in all. They are all, that is, eschatological. That requires some explanation.

To say that the church is eschatological is to say that it is provisional and not absolute. This was something a small minority of the Council Fathers were reluctant to say, but the vast majority were more than happy to say. The church is provisional in this present age; she "will attain her full perfection only in the glory of heaven."[38]

The church, as I noted earlier, is but a moon revolving around Christ, the sun and the light of the world (John 8:12). While the sun remains constant, the moon waxes and wanes, shining brightly when it draws near the sun, becoming darkness when it moves away from it. Because of this constant waxing and waning, the church is always in need of renewal, it is *ecclesia semper reformanda.* "Christ summons the church," the Council teaches, "to that continual reformation of which she always has need, insofar as she is an institution of men here on earth."[39] So will it be until the moon is so completely irradiated by the light of its sun that it will be indistinguishable from it.

As the "universal sacrament of salvation,"[40] the church has to be provisional, for a sacrament is essentially something provisional. In sacraments, the Grace that saves is made explicit in the world, but only, as Aquinas once said in a sadly forgotten hymn, as *pignus futurae gloriae,* as a pledge of future glory. In the end, both church and sacraments will give way to the God and the grace they now symbolize. There should be no difficulty, the Fathers argued, in allowing that the church is provisional, for all sacramental symbols are provisional. They will all give way sooner or later to the reality they symbolize. Paul's formulation of the difference between symbol and reality still says it best: "Now we see in a mirror (symbol) dimly, but then face to face" (1 Cor.12:12).

The church is provisional, however, not in the sense that it will vanish one day without trace, but in the sense that it will be transfigured ultimately into the heavenly reality it now symbolizes. As Christ, its head, was transformed from an earthly body into a heavenly one (cf. 1 Cor.15:35-41), so too will the church, his sacramental Body, be transformed. Until that definitive moment of glory, it will remain a pilgrim people, "genuinely but imperfectly holy,"[41] making its way in faith and hope and love toward its final transformation. "Faith," the church confesses in the Letter to the Hebrews, "is the assurance of things hoped for, the conviction of things not seen" (11:1). When faith gives way to vision, so will the faithful church give way to the triune God it now represents. Then, finally, God will be all in all (1 Cor.15:28). Until that moment, the church remains a people on its pilgrim way.

In his earthly existence, Jesus of Nazareth was a Jewish preacher who preached the kingdom of God (Mark 1:15). This kingdom is not to be conceived as a territory or as a sphere of dominion, as is, for instance, the kingdom of England. *Malkuth Yahweh* is a much more dynamic reality than that. It is nothing less than God's active rule in our world, nothing less than the reign of God, as modern translations of the New Testament now render it. We can go further and say that kingdom of God is an image for the active presence of God among his People. This kingdom-presence,

Lumen Gentium teaches, "is clearly visible in the very person of Christ . . . who came 'to serve and to give his life as a ransom for many' (Mark 10:45)."[42]

Those who believed in God's kingdom-presence in Jesus, and who especially believed in it in his death and resurrection, felt themselves called to be the Lord's gathering, the communion of faith, the *ekklesia*, the church. They felt called to be, as Jesus was, the servant of the kingdom and of the presence of God. The church, therefore, is not absolute; it is not for itself. It is not the presence of God, but the servant of Presence. It is not grace, but the minister of Grace. It is not the kingdom of God, though the kingdom of God ought to be its impulse. The church is not absolute, it is not for itself. It is only the sacrament of Christ and of his God, and that only until he comes. The church is incontestably eschatological.

Theological Reflection

The outcome of the deliberations on church at the Second Vatican Council was a strong insistence on the fact that the church is a mystery, and therefore something of which we cannot speak directly. We can speak of it only indirectly in images, as does the New Testament. Several theologians, both before and since the Council, have drawn attention to the multiplicity of biblical images for the church, and they have pointed out that the profusion of images is a sign not of logical confusion but of theological life.[43]

In his influential *Models of the Church,* Avery Dulles sought to offer a critical assessment of the church in all its aspects, including its images.[44] Judging that all images of the church, precisely because they are images of mystery, are open to not only valid and useful but also invalid and destructive applications, he elected to underscore the exploratory or heuristic nature of images as models. Such an approach insists, correctly, that images, both concrete images like People, Body, Servant, Herald, and highly abstract images like Institution, Community, Sacrament, are not exact replications of mystery, but signposts to insight into mystery. They are intended to challenge and inspire believers to deeper understanding and to action appropriate to that understanding.

If Congar is right in his insistence that a theology of ministry reflects an underlying theology of church, and I repeat that I have no doubt that he is, then corresponding to a profusion of models of church is an equal profusion of models of ministry. As the underlying image or model of church changes, the image or model of ministry tied to it also changes. Before setting out, therefore, to consider church and ministry in some detail, we would do well to heed Dulles' wise warning. "It should be scarcely necessary to point out that no good ecclesiologist is exclusively committed to a single model of the church,"[45] nor exclusively committed to a single model of ministry either.

But we need to be realistic. Divisions abound in the church today because of over-commitment to one model rather than to another. They are permanent signs of the permanent need to heed Dulles' warning. It was precisely the Preparatory Commission's over-commitment to one model of the church, the institutional model, that produced the document that the Council found so wanting. It was precisely the commitment to a profusion of images and models that led it to *Lumen Gentium,* a quite different document.

The underlying model which will control my vision throughout this book is the one which Vatican II elected to make its underlying model, and which the 1985 Extraordinary Synod declared to be "the central and fundamental idea of the Council's documents."[46] The church is the communion of "the new People of God."[47] I will borrow Pope John Paul II's specification of that community. "If we wish to be conscious of this community of the People of God, we must first contemplate Christ saying to each member of the community, 'Follow me'. It is a community of disciples, each of whom in some way . . . is following Christ."

Both the underlying model, communion of the People of God, and its specification, communion of disciples, are biblical images. The former emphasizes the essentially communal nature of the church, not only the vertical communion of each believer with the trinitarian God, but also the horizontal communion of each with the other. The latter suggests that being a member of Christ's church is not a static condition to be maintained but a dynamic task to be achieved.

Disciple is an important New Testament word, occurring some two hundred and fifty times throughout the Gospels and the Acts and always implying response to a call from Jesus. By definition, disciples are learners, and the disciples of Christ are learners of Mystery. They gather in response to his call to seek insight together into a triple mystery: the mystery of the great God of Israel, who seeks to be known and loved by them; the mystery of Jesus whom this God raised from the dead and made Lord and Christ (Acts 2:24,36); the mystery of the communion in which they gather and which is called and is the Body of Christ. They are summoned to insight, not only in theory but also in practice, for they are called not only to Christian understanding, but also to Christian action (cf. Matt.7:21-23). The fact that the church is a communion of disciples and that the practical cost of discipleship is high is, at least, one of the reasons for the sad reality that faces all the Christian churches today, the reality of the baptized non-believer.[49]

Too much has been made in recent Christian history of baptism as a ritual which "makes" a person a Christian, irrespective of personal dispositions. Not enough has been made, on the other hand, of the necessity of personal, as distinct from merely institutional, initiation into the communion of disciples and of formation in and into its faith. John Paul II cites with approval the wise words of the Synod on the Laity. Christian formation is "a continual process in the individual of maturation in faith and a likening to Christ." That formation of the lay faithful, he insists, is to be placed among the priorities of every diocese.[50]

Baptized non-believers are those who have been baptized, frequently in infancy and therefore impersonally, but who have never been personally formed in and into faith, "without which it is impossible to please God (Heb.11:6) and to be counted as his sons."[51] Because of baptism, they are institutionally and technically believers, Christians, church, but lacking personal faith, they are personally non-believers, non-Christians, non-church. They ought never to be equated with believers and with church just because they *physically* underwent a water ritual.

The new *Code of Canon Law* attempts to take account of the importance of personal faith. Only those baptized are in full communion with the Catholic Church, it prescribes, "who are joined with Christ in his visible body through the bonds of *profession of faith*."[52] This is no more than the most recent legal assertion of something which has been the tradition of the Christian church. That tradition has been constant from the insistence of Jesus on the necessity of personal faith (cf. Matt.9:22; 9:29;15:28; 17:20; 21:21), to his complaints about its absence (Matt.6:30; 8:26; 14:31; 16:8; 17:20), to Paul's vehement defense of the necessity of faith against the Judaizers (Rom.3:28 and passim; Gal.2:16 and passim), to the proclamation of the Council of Trent noted above, to the equally firm teaching of the Second Vatican Council that sacraments "not only presuppose faith" but "also nourish and strengthen it," which "is why they are called 'sacraments of faith'."[53]

No man or woman is justified without personal faith. No longer can it be taken for granted that Christians are initiated into a passive church in which all that is required of them is that they be baptized. They are initiated into an active communion of disciples, believing in Christ and seeking to learn in practice to heed his invitation: "You go into the vineyard too" (Matt. 20:4). In all that follows, when I say *church,* I shall intend such a communion of baptized, believing, ministering disciples.

Summary

In this chapter, I have sought to underscore the renewed vision of church given to the Christian community by the Second Vatican Council. This vision presents the church as a mystery, that is, "a reality impregnated with the presence of God and, therefore, of such a nature that there are ever-new and deeper explorations of it possible."[54] These deeper explorations led us to the trinitarian innerness of the church, to its nature as People of God and sacrament of Christ, to its character as a dynamic communion of disciples, actively seeking to discover what it means in theory and in practice to believe in Christ. They led us to the realization that the church is not a passive communion of believers but a very active one, and that believing in Jesus is never only something to be said but also many things to be done. Among those things is ministry, which I shall define in the next chapter and unfold in the rest of this book.

Questions for Reflection

1. What implications do you see in the change from an exclusive focus on the church as an hierarchical society to a focus which includes also the church as People of God and as communion of disciples? Do you believe that it is necessary for every single person to conceive the church in the same way? Why?

2. How do you understand the statement that the church is mystery? What challenges and inspiration do you see in a church that is mystery?

3. What does sacrament mean to you? What does it mean in practice to say that the church is the sacrament of salvation and the sacrament of unity in the world?

4. What do you understand by the phrase *baptized non-believer*? What would be the difference(s) between a baptized believer and a baptized non-believer?

5. What do you understand by the statement that the church is eschatological? Does that understanding contribute anything to your understanding of church?

Suggested Reading

Dogmatic Constitution on the Church, in *The Documents of Vatican II*, ed. Walter M. Abbott (New York: Herder and Herder, 1966).

Carmody, Denise L. *Bonded in Christ's Love: An Introduction to Ecclesiology* (New York: Paulist, 1986).

Dulles, Avery. *Models of the Church* (New York: Doubleday, 1974).

Dulles, Avery. *A Church to Believe In: Discipleship and the Dynamics of Freedom* (New York: Crossroad, 1982).

Kress, Robert. *The Church: Communion, Sacrament, Communication.* (New York: Paulist, 1985).

Minear, Paul. *Images of the Church in the New Testament* (Philadelphia: Westminster Press, 1960).

Segundo, Juan. *The Community Called Church* (New York: Orbis, 1973).

2.

Church and Ministry

Church and Ministry

If the preaching *of* Jesus was centered on the kingdom-presence of God, the preaching *about* Jesus was centered on the fact that God raised him from the dead (cf. 1 Cor.15:4; Acts 2:24). Jesus the preacher gave way to Jesus the preached. Much of Jesus' preaching had sounded blasphemous in pious Israelite ears. But the earliest preaching about him proclaimed that he had been raised from the dead and thus confirmed by the God of Israel. The belief that the crucified preacher had been raised by God gave rise to a theology which saw in him the righteous one (Acts 3:14; 7:52; 22:14), the Lord and Christ established in power (Acts 2:36), who calls and sends disciples to carry on his proclamation of the kingdom-presence of God (Matt. 28:16-20).

The New Testament remembers the confusion that surrounded the identity of Jesus. "Who do they say that I am?," he asks. John the Baptizer, they respond, or Elijah or one of the prophets (cf. Mark 8:27; Matt.16:13-14). The earliest preaching, though, sets the record straight: "You are the Christ, the Son of the living God" (Matt.16:16). But that answer, as Paul well realized, hinges on belief in his resurrection. For "if Christ has not been raised, then our preaching is in vain and your faith is in vain" (1 Cor.15:14). God's raising of Jesus from the dead, that is, in the Jewish parlance of the times, her recreating him and bringing him to herself, is the definitive clue which dispels the confusion about the identity both of Jesus and of the God whose kingdom-presence he proclaims.

The resurrection of Jesus is the act that proclaims, makes explicit and celebrates the ultimate meaning of his person, his words and his deeds. That meaning, at the intersection of humanity and divinity, is twofold. On the one hand, the resurrection proclaims that Jesus can be trusted, for he has been vouched for by the great God of Israel. On the other hand, it proclaims that the God to whose kingdom-presence the person and the words and the deeds of Jesus point can also be trusted, for she raised the righteous Jesus from the dead and brought him to herself.

Central to the memory of Jesus is the recollection that he was completely obedient to God. Yet God did not protect him as she ought to have done. But, as Donald Dawe points out in a recent book,[55] to say with the New Testament that Jesus died according to the "deliberate plan and foreknowledge of God" (Acts 2:23) is to say that, in the death of Jesus, God transcended all previous conceptions of her. When Jesus died, the Protector-God of every human desire died too. When Jesus was raised from the dead, God was revealed as the One who makes new.

Such is the vision and the hope, of both humanity and divinity, that Christianity holds out to men and women. Beyond past and present sin, the God who is in Jesus can make all things new. Even death, Jesus' resurrection makes clear, is not beyond the power of God. John glimpsed this message of transformation at the beginning of the Christian movement. "We are God's children now," he says; but "it does not yet appear what we shall be."[66] Only one thing is clear: "we shall be like her" (1 John 3:2), that is, made new, as was Jesus.

As Pannenberg would have it, Jesus is the *prolepsis* of both the human and the divine, the person of the future inserted into the present. He is the end before the end. In him the shape of the future of both humankind and God has already appeared in human history. To believe in Jesus, and in the God he reveals, is to share in that future now and to be drawn forward to see both the human and the divine as they will be. It is to such a vision and such a hope, and to a ministry founded in both, that the Christian church is called.

Not only was Jesus raised from the dead by God, but also "he was made manifest to Cephas, then to the twelve" (1 Cor. 15:5). This being *made manifest, appeared* as it is in the pre-modern versions of the New Testament, has an incontrovertible source. As the God of Israel raised Jesus from the dead, so also she made him manifest to selected witnesses. These witnesses were called to believe Jesus' resurrection on the basis of this divine manifestation, or revelation as Paul chose to call it (Gal.1:15-16). Everyone else is called to believe it on the testimony of these witnesses and declared blessed, not if they have seen, but if they have believed (John 20:29). Those who did believe experienced themselves as called by God to be his gathered people, his *ekklesia*, his church. As Alfred Loisy once said, with more positive intent than is usually ascribed to him, "Jesus announced the kingdom of God, and what arrived was the church."[56]

The New Testament is the record of that church's understanding, not only of Jesus and of the kingdom he preached, but also of itself. The central kerygma in the record is that God raised Jesus from the dead (1 Cor.15:3-4; Rom.8:34; Gal.1:1; Eph.1:20; Acts 2:24), and made him head of a body which is the church (1 Cor.6:12-20; 10:17; 12:12-27; Rom 12:4-5; Eph. 1:22-23; 2:14-16; 3:6; 4:4-16; 5:22-30; Col.1:18, 24; 2:19; 3:15). The record declares universally that members of the church are "in Christ" and it explains how they got to be in Christ and to be one body. "As many of you as were baptized into Christ have put on Christ. There is neither Jew nor Greek, there is neither slave nor free, there is neither male nor female; for you are all one person in Christ Jesus" (Gal.3:27-28). Believers somehow become both in Christ and the Body of Christ in the ritual of baptism. But for most of us, I believe, that *somehow* needs careful elaboration.

For the ancient Semite, both Arab and Jew, water was an element to the whim of which men and women were constantly subject. Because of this subjection, water was celebrated in their most ancient mythologies. The Babylonian *Enuma Elish*, in which creation is described as the activity of the great god of Babylon, Marduk, overcoming and putting in order the chaos that is Tiamat-Sea, is the most detailed of such mythological accounts. But elements of the chaotic water motif are found also in the

Jewish account of creation in Genesis 1. In the beginning, we read, "the earth was without form and void, and darkness was upon the face of *tehom*" (1:2). If *tehom*, the watery deep, is not exactly identical to Tiamat-Sea, it is at least a remnant of that mythical personification of sea.

An even clearer remnant is found in the Book of Job, where we learn that "with her power (God) stilled Sea, with her skill she smote Rahab (a mythical seamonster), with her wind she bagged Sea" (26:12-13). Yahweh, the great God of Israel, like Marduk the great god of Babylon, is represented as creating by putting chaotic water in its place. She creates, not out of Greek nothingness, but out of Semitic primordial water. Unfortunately, however, creation does not exhaust her activity with water. For there are other mythological narratives, the Babylonian *Gilgamesh Epic* and the Jewish account of the great flood, which present the great God as letting water rage forth again to bring death. The very same primordial water is an ambivalent and a powerful symbol. It represents both life and death.

If water is such an omnipresent symbol in mythology, it is predictable that it will be a prominent symbol also in ritual. And, of course, it is, both in Judaism and in Christianity. The occasion for the Jewish water rite of passage, *tebilah,* is the conversion of Gentiles to Judaism, the passage from one cultural condition (being a Gentile) to another (being a Jew).[57] Before they can become Jews, Gentiles must be separated from their Gentile state. What better way to do this than to return them, at least in ritual, to the water of chaotic non-being. So they were immersed in water to become again, as in the beginning, "without form and void." Then the Spirit of Yahweh, again, as in the beginning, swept over the water and from it again brought new life. The once and former Gentiles were returned, ritually, to their original nothingness, to be brought forth again by Yahweh to new life as a now and future Jew.

The occasion for Christian baptism is the conversion to belief in Jesus the Christ. When faced with the question of how to become like this Christ, who died and was raised from the dead, the first Semitic believers reached back into their water symbolisms. To become like Christ, they would have to do what he did, namely, go down into death and be raised

again to new life. What better way to effect this and to celebrate it than to
be immersed in the waters of ritual death and from there be raised again by
God? What better way, in short, than to be baptized? So baptized they
were.

In the early Syrian church, the emphasis in this ritual fell on new birth,
as in born "of water and the Spirit" (John 3:5). In the earlier Palestinian
church, it fell on death and resurrection, as in "were buried with him by
baptism into death, so that as Christ was raised from the dead by the glory
of the Father, we too might walk in newness of life" (Rom.6:4). That these
two interpretations quickly came together is clear from the baptismal
catecheses of Cyril of Jerusalem, who explains to the newly-baptized that
"in the very same moment you were both dead and born, and that saving
water became both tomb and mother (womb) to you."[58]

In baptism, then, Christians are ritually born again. As God raised Jesus
from death to new life and anointed him as *Christos,* so also she transforms
those who are baptized from not-Christian to Christian and anoints them as
christos. But, for all its wonder, the ritual birth achieved in baptism is not
enough. Too much weight can be and, in recent centuries has been, placed
on baptism, as if immersion in water was all that was necessary to become
Christian. But baptism is only a beginning. Becoming Christian requires
more than baptism, it requires also a Christ-like life.

Cyprian, the third-century bishop of Carthage, always concerned with
baptismal life, is in no doubt. Putting on Christ in baptism is quite meaningless unless baptism is followed by a Christ-like life. "To put on the
name of Christ and not continue along the way of Christ, what is that but a
lie?"[59] If we have put him on, we "ought to go forward according to the
example of Christ."[60] John Paul II is asserting the same thing in contemporary theological language when he says that "communion and mission
are profoundly connected with one another, they interpenetrate and
mutually imply each other. Communion gives rise to mission, and mission
is accomplished in communion."[61] Which returns us to the elect communion which is the church.

The church is the church of God (1 Cor.1:2; 10:32; 11:16, 22; 15:9; 2 Cor. 1:1; Gal. 1:13; 1 Thess. 2:14; 2 Thess. 1:4; 1 Tim 3:5; Acts 20:28), but also the church of Christ (Rom.16:16). It is those men and women who have been called by God to believe in her presence in Jesus and who have responded to that call by bonding themselves in baptism to live in communion with Christ and with one another. Christ's church is essentially a communion.

The communion that is the church is a "kind of sacrament,"[62] both a sign and an instrument of the Christ and of the presence-kingdom he serves. It is a symbol which proclaims, makes explicit and celebrates in the world the Christ and the presence-kingdom of God.[63] As a sacramental communion, the church is two-tiered. On one level, it is a communion of men and women bonded together by their belief in Jesus whom they confess as the Christ. On another level, it is a communion which is a symbol of the Christ and of the God he reveals.

The communion called church, as we have seen, is ritually born in the waters of baptism. It is sustained and further fashioned as communion of the members with Christ and with one another in the ritual meal called eucharist. This meal is the symbol of communion, in the sense that it both proclaims and makes explicit church communion. Communion in the eucharistic Body of Christ signifies and builds up communion in the church, which is also the Body of Christ. As Paul explained to the Corinthians, "we who are many are one body, for we all partake of the one bread" (1 Cor.10:17). Ignatius of Antioch so valued the "one bread" that he exhorted the Philadelphians "to observe *one* eucharist. For there is one flesh of our Lord, Jesus Christ, and one cup of his blood that makes us one."[64]

This understanding of the central role of eucharist as symbol of the church's communion was continued at Rome. There, for centuries after the inauguration of Sunday eucharists, fragments of the bread consecrated at the bishop's eucharist were sent to be placed in the cups at all other eucharists, joining all together in one eucharist and one symbol of the one church.[65] It is tempting to reflect on the effect of many eucharists, which divide the church both in fact and in symbol. But the present context neither permits nor requires such a diversion. Here I wish only to underscore the essential communion of the church and the function of the eucharist as the central sacrament, that is, the central sign and means, of that communion.

The church is the sacramental symbol of Christ in the world. But Christ is the minister, the servant, the deacon (Mark 10:45) in the world of God and of her presence-kingdom. The church, therefore, must be the minister, the servant, the deacon of the same God and of the same kingdom. To repeat once more, the commitment to Christ in baptism must be followed by a Christ-like life. The church is not for itself; nor is its ministry for itself. The church is not the absolute presence of God, but the minister of her Presence. It is not absolute grace, but the servant of Grace. It is not the kingdom of God, but only the servant of the Kingdom. It ministers and serves and deacons (at least in Greek that is a verb) specifically by incarnating in its life in the world the Christ and the God he serves. The call to be church is, of necessity, the call to a servant life.[66]

In the New Testament churches, ministry is an ecclesial function. There are individual ministers, a great variety of them, ranging from the apostles, prophets and teachers which we find in the genuinely Pauline churches (cf. 1 Cor.12:4-12, 28; Rom. 12:4-8; Eph.4:11-14), to the overseers (*episkopoi*), presbyters (*presbyteroi*) and deacons (*diakonoi*), which we find in the Deutero-Pauline Letters. The latter triad, as is well known, became the exclusive referent of the term *ministry* in the Roman Empire and, therefore, also in the Roman Catholic church.

How ministry came to be associated exclusively with overseers, presbyters and deacons remains quite unclear. What is clear is both *that* it did and *that* the exclusivity created a serious misunderstanding of ministry. The leadership ministries of overseers, presbyters and deacons, ministries though they undoubtedly are, are not simply *the ministry*. That judgment is so well accepted in the Roman Catholic Church that Vatican II was moved to make a substantial change in an important teaching of the Council of Trent. The change is of the greatest import for a theology of ministry and ministers.

Trent had taught this. "If anyone says that there is not, by divine ordination (*divina ordinatione*) in the Catholic church a hierarchy which is
composed (*constat*) of bishops, priests and ministers (*ministris*), let him be
anathema."[67] To bring this teaching into line with the unquestioned, because unquestionable, historical evidence, Vatican II changed it to read as
follows. "The divinely established ecclesiastical ministry (*ministerium ec-
clesiasticum*) is exercised on different levels by those who from antiquity
(*ab antiquo*, not *ab initio*) have been called bishops, priests and
deacons."[68]

The replacement of *hierarchy* with *ecclesiastical ministry* is a critical
change. It was intended to emphasize that it is the ministry of the church,
and not the hierarchical form of that ministry, which is of divine estab-
lishment. Acknowledging the historical fact that, from the beginning, ministry in the church was pluriform, this declaration loosens the exclusive
connection of ministry to hierarchy and restores the idea that ministry is an
ecclesial function, exercised by all those who serve on behalf of the
church.

Luke opens his account of the ministry of Jesus with a pregnant quota-
tion from Isaiah. "The Spirit of the Lord is upon me. . . . She has *sent* me to
proclaim release to the captives, recovering of sight to the blind and to set
at liberty those that are oppressed" (4:18-19; see also 4:43 and John 3:16-
17; 5:36-37; 6:28-29; 7:29; 8:18; 12:49). The gospel Jesus has a strong
sense of having been sent, and having been sent specifically to serve. "If
anyone would be first," he explains to his disciples, "he must be the last of
all and the *diakonos-servant* of all" (Mark 9:35; cf. Matt. 20:26-27; Luke
22:26-27; Acts 3:26). To James and John, who seek places of honor, he
specifically explains that "whoever would be first among you must be the
servant (*doulos*) of all. For the Son of Man came not to be served but to
serve" (Mark 10:44-45).

The church, which is the sacrament-symbol of Jesus in the world can be
no more or no less than he. Ministry in the church must be *diakonia,* service; ministers in the church must be *diakonoi,* servants. Power in the
church must be the power that is service and that derives from service.
Like the Christ whose sacrament and body it is, the church is a servant

church. Whoever is called to ministry in the church is called to be a servant. I shall explain in a moment that, in general, it and they serve by incarnating, that is, by embodying, by making explicit and by celebrating in symbol, the presence in the world of the Christ and of the God who sent him to serve.

Ministry Defined

In the Fall of 1987, Cardinal Hume, the Archbishop of Westminster, reported to the Synod on the Laity that one of the pressing needs in any discussion of ministry today is "greater clarity in the use of the term." He suggested that the designation *ministry* should be applied only to service in the name of a church community and authorized by a bishop.[69] He was right in demanding clarity, for in the contemporary church *ministry* is being used indiscriminately to describe almost anything that Christians do. Such indiscriminate use cheapens the reality to which the term refers. When everything is described as ministry, then the word loses definition and becomes meaningless, and nothing is distinguishably ministry. I intend now to respond to Cardinal Hume's request by setting forth a definition of ministry.

A word of warning, however, is always appropriate as an introduction to a definition. Definitions not only clarify but also, and of necessity, delimit; they not only include some things in but they also include some things out. I understand that and, for the sake of specificity, I intend it. The warning delivered, here is the definition: ministry is action done in public, on behalf of the church, as a result of a charism of service, proclaimed, made explicit and celebrated in the church in sacrament, to incarnate in symbol the presence of Christ and of the God whose kingdom he reveals.[70] A clarification of the terms of this definition is in order.

Ministry is action. But it is intended action, not just accidental action. It is action which is the result of planning. Christians are baptized, as we saw, into an active communion of service, not into a passive one. They are called and sent, not to chant a mantric "Lord, Lord," but to do "the will of my Father" (Matt. 7:21; Luke 6:46) in service. Aquinas was right, however, *agere sequitur esse,* action flows from being. To be *Christian* ministry, therefore, action must flow from Christian being, from the belief in and the commitment to represent Jesus, the Christ.

In the earliest Christian churches, such ministry was designated by ordinary words describing actions done to spread the Christian gospel. These words, teach, preach, prophesy, serve, reconcile, heal, lead, oversee, and a myriad others, are responsive words. The actions they designate are actions in response to needs. Action though it be, ministry is never action for the sake of action; it is always action in response to need. Later in Christian history, the words which originally designated action in response to need became institutionalized to designate ministerial offices in the churches, whether they continued to respond to needs or not.

Ministry is not only action; it is also action *in public.* Those who believe in Jesus as the Christ are called to be church and are sent to serve the presence of God in the world by living a Christ-like life. They are called, for instance, to prayer and patient suffering, to self-sacrifice, to love and to joy. But none of this, thoroughly Christian though it be, is Christian ministry. If the church in Jerusalem had ministered simply by loving prayer and joyful long-suffering, there might have been a church in Jerusalem today, but there would have been none anywhere else.

I hope not to be misunderstood here. I am not saying that prayer and suffering are in no way a service to the church, for they are. I am saying only that they are not to be designated as Christian ministry. They might fuel ministry; they might eventually lead to ministry. But they are not, of themselves, the prime analogate for Christian ministry. For Christian ministry is not just service in the church, but *public* service.

In the climactic conclusion to Matthew's gospel, Jesus' disciples are sent to teach and to baptize and to make more disciples. That indicates the public character of their ministry. Paul describes himself as called and sent "to be a minister (*leitourgos*) of Christ Jesus to the Gentiles" (Rom. 15:16). *Leitourgos* is a common Greek word designating a public official who performs a *leitourgia* or public office.

Webster notes that *public* derives from the Latin *populus*-people and that it has a variety of meanings. I wish to underscore only two of them: first, acting in an official capacity on behalf of the people, as in *public* prosecutor; secondly, acting in a way apt to be known by all or most of the people, as in made *public*. Ultimately, what I mean by action in public is well exemplified by what we find from beginning to end in the Acts of the Apostles. There we find the apostles "every day in the temple and at home . . . teaching and preaching Jesus the Christ" (5:42), and we find Paul in Rome "preaching the kingdom of God and teaching about the Lord Jesus Christ quite openly" (28:31).

That last is, perhaps, the key. Christian ministry is service which is carried out openly, in public, as a public official, not in private as a private individual. Such public activity not only may, but also must, be fueled by private activities such as prayer and patient suffering. But such private activities are not Christian ministry. When everything is described as ministry, as I said, then nothing is distinguishably ministry. That is a recipe for disaster, which I believe is detectable in much of the contemporary discussion and practice of Christian ministry. It is to obviate such disaster that I wish to define ministry as, and limit it to, action in public.

Ministry is action done in public, but not every action done in public is ministry. Only that action done *on behalf of the Christian church* and on behalf of its mission is Christian ministry. It is now well-known and freely acknowledged that neither in the New Testament nor in the immediate post-apostolic church is the word *hiereus,* priest, used to designate any Christian minister. But the priestly element, so much to the fore in Judaism, did not disappear without trace. It was transmuted to express, first, the role of Christ and, then, the role of the church. I shall defer treatment of these facts until the next chapter. Here, I shall content myself by asserting that specific Christian ministry begins in the church and flows out from it in mission to sustain and expand in explicit reality the kingdom of God.

The church's needs are varied, and the ministries required to respond to them are, of necessity, also varied. Since there are many services required in the church, there are required also many ministries. Preachers serve by proclaiming the word of God; teachers serve by explaining it; prophets serve by telling it in concrete circumstances. Ministers of all kinds serve by translating it into structures of justice and peace, and into care for the poor and the dispossessed, for the sick and the imprisoned. Ministers specifically ordained for leadership serve by leading the church, the Body of Christ, into communion with and imitation of the Christ. All are servants of the word, and of the presence, of the grace and of the kingdom of God it proclaims.[71] All ministers, that is, are essentially deacons, whether or not they hold that ordained office.

Sometimes they are deacons who look inward, to serve and to challenge, and thereby to sustain, the church. Sometimes they are deacons who look outward, to invite men and women into the presence and the kingdom of God, thereby expanding the church. But whether they look inwards or outwards they are deacons, not as isolated individuals, but always as members of, and acting on behalf of, a Christian church. For Christians, the church community, precisely as the sacramental incarnation of Christ, is at the heart of Christian ministry.

The word *charisma,* charism, was introduced into theological terminology by Paul. In its root Greek form, *charis,* it means gift in general, but in Paul and in the tradition which followed him, it means specifically a gift of the Holy Spirit that impels a believer to the service of the church. Writing to the Corinthians, Paul enumerates a great variety of such gifts, knowledge, wisdom, faith, miracles, prophecy, healing, teaching, speaking in tongues, discernment (1 Cor. 12:8-10, 28:30; cf. Rom. 12:6-8; Eph. 4:11).

There are two important characteristics of charism to be noted. First, it is a gift of the Spirit which is given freely to a person, not one given as a reward for good behavior or as a result of office. This is the constant teaching of the church which has always agreed with Paul's teaching that "No one can say 'Jesus is Lord' except by the Holy Spirit" (1 Cor.12:3). Secondly, charism is "for the common good" (1 Cor. 12:7), "for the work of ministry, for the building up of the Body of Christ" (Eph. 4:12). Because and in so far as the church is the Body of Christ, because and in so far as Christ's Spirit moves each member of the church to service, and because and in so far as Christ himself is present in each gift and in each service which it creates, "to this extent it can be proclaimed in truth that he fills all things with the power of his resurrection."[72]

Since "charisms are graces of the Holy Spirit that have, directly or indirectly, a usefulness for the ecclesial community, ordered as they are to the building up of the church,"[73] their recipients are obligated, and therefore have the right, to use them for the good of church communion and mission. Such use was well-known and legitimate in the earliest church communities. But as ministry in the church became more and more institutionalized, charismatic ministry was more and more absorbed into hierarchical ministry, eventually vanishing almost entirely.[74] Perhaps that is why John Paul II, in his Apostolic Exhortation on the Laity, insinuates an unwarranted distinction between ministries and charisms, as if ministries were not themselves gifts of the Holy Spirit.[75]

The behavior of the Spirit of God today, again distributing her gifts where she freely wills, clarifies what should have been always obvious, namely, that charisms, including the charism of ministry, are not the exclusive possession of ordained ministers. The Second Vatican Council was merely acknowledging this fact when it taught that the Spirit "distributes special graces among the faithful of every rank," making them thereby "fit and ready to undertake the various tasks or offices advantageous for the renewal and the upbuilding of the church."[76] Charism is again rampant and acknowledged in the church, not only the ecstatic charisms associated with glossolalia, but also those more restrained and ordinary ones which named tasks needed for the upbuilding of the church long before they named offices. Christians proclaim and make explicit and celebrate such gifts in sacraments.

To serve clarity, another definition is needed here, the definition of sacrament. I have dealt extensively with that definition elsewhere. Here I wish only to state it. "A sacrament is a prophetic symbol, established by and modeled upon Christ the symbol of God, in and by which the church, the Body of Christ, proclaims, realizes and celebrates that presence and action of God, which is rightly called grace."[77] Sacramentality is an essential characteristic of the catholic traditions. They always proclaim, make explicit and celebrate in sacrament the mysterious grace of the God and Savior in whom they steadfastly believe. They always mark the points of intersection of the human and the divine with sacrament. It is at those points that ministries exist.

The catholic sacramental tradition derives from the same root as everything else that is Christian; it derives from the man, Jesus of Nazareth. By being, on one level, a man who, on another level, is confessed as the embodiment or the incarnation of God, and by calling into being a communion of believers who, on one level, are men and women and, on another level, are proclaimed as the embodiment of Christ, Jesus set patterns for sacramental realization. The church follows these patterns in its actions, so that when it acts, especially when its acts formally and solemnly, its actions are not just the actions of men and women but also the actions of Christ and of the God he reveals.

The actions of the church are sacramental actions. On one level, they appear to be quite simple human actions: immersion in water, anointing with oil, laying on of hands. But, on another level, they are far from simple actions. They are symbolic actions, proclaiming and making explicit and celebrating belief in the Christ who was dead and who was raised to life, the incorporation of believers into the Body of that Christ, and their ordination to ministry in that Body. The sacraments of initiation proclaim and make explicit and celebrate the charisms of non-ordained ministry. The sacrament of ordination does the same for the charisms of ordained ministry.

"Jesus the Christ came into Galilee, preaching the good news of God and saying 'The time is fulfilled and the kingdom of God is at hand'" (Mark 1:14-15). That kingdom, as I have insisted, is an image for the gracious presence of God in human history, and it is this kingdom as gracious presence that Jesus serves. For the men and women of our world, that presence is ambiguous. Jesus serves it by proclaiming it, by making it explicit and by celebrating it in his person, in his words and in his deeds. He serves it, as the theological tradition has always insisted, by incarnating it in the world.

That is how the church, which claims to be his Body, also serves. In its concrete presence, in its concrete words, in its concrete actions in public, the church serves the kingdom and the presence of God by proclaiming them, by making them explicit, and by celebrating them. The church serves the kingdom by incarnating it. Its ministry is always at the point of intersection of the human and the divine. It is always a ministry of incarnation—of Christ and of the presence of the God he serves.

Summary

This chapter sought to define the term *ministry* and to clarify its connection to the church and to the Christ, whose Body the church is. It characterized the church as essentially a ministerial and servant church, and ministry, therefore, as essentially servant activity. Like Jesus, the church and its various ministers serve by incarnating in the world the presence of the Christ and of the God he incarnates. I shall detail further distinctions in the church and in its ministries in each succeeding chapter.

Questions for Reflection

1. Reflect on Paul's kerygma "that he was buried, that he was raised on the third day in accordance with the scriptures, and that he *was made manifest* (*opthe*) to Cephas, then to the twelve" (1 Cor. 15:4-5). How do you understand the term *was made manifest*? How do you understand the claim that God's raising of Jesus and her making him manifest is her summons to a communion called church?

2. What implications for Christian living are involved in the claim that membership in the church is membership in an essentially ministerial communion?

3. Does the definition of ministry clarify the notion for you in any way? Do you agree that ecclesial ministry derived from initiation into the Christian church is as much Christian ministry as that derived from ordination?

4. How do you understand that part of the definition which says that all the ministries of the church are ministries of incarnation of Christ and of the God he serves?

5. What do you understand by the theological word *charism*? Can you name any charisms the Holy Spirit has given to you? What do you believe they are for?

Suggested Reading

Cooke, Bernard. *Ministry to Word and Sacraments* (Philadelphia: Fortress, 1977).

Küng, Hans (ed.). *The Plurality of Ministries* (New York: Herder and Herder, 1972).

Lutherans and Catholics in Dialogue, Vol.IV: Eucharist and Ministry (Washington: USCC, 1970).

MacQuarrie, John. *Theology, Church and Ministry* (London: SCM, 1986).

O'Meara, Thomas F. *Theology of Ministry* (New York: Paulist, 1983).

3.

Laity in the Church

According to the Second Vatican Council, the term *laity* refers to "all the faithful except those in holy orders and those in a religious state sanctioned by the church."[78] It is surprising that, thirty years after Yves Congar's plea that laity not continue to be defined negatively, not-a-cleric, not-a-religious,[79] the only definition of laity the Council at which he had such an enormous influence could offer was precisely that negative one. Even more surprising, however, is the fact that the definition would have made no sense in any of the New Testament churches. For at that time there was no such thing as laity nor, for that matter, any such thing as cleric. I shall defer treatment of the latter fact until the next chapter, and here deal only with the fact that there was no laity.

People of God

In the great covenant ratification ceremony in Israel, "all the people answered together and said, 'All that the Lord has spoken we will do'" (Ex. 19:8; cf. Ex. 24:3; Joshua 24:21). *The people* gave their answer to the God who had said to them: "You shall be to me a kingdom of priests and a holy people" (Ex. 19:6). When Christians began to reflect on the meaning of their separate movement, they expressed it in terms borrowed from these covenant texts. They perceived themselves as "a chosen race, a royal priesthood, a holy people" (1 Pet. 2:9). The self-understanding of both Israel and Christianity, its off-shoot, is a collective, communal understanding, a sense of being a unified people before God. For both religions everything else depends on and takes its meaning from that one fact of peoplehood.

The Greek word for people is *laos*. This ordinary word came to be applied to the Christian church, which is described as *laos theou*, the People of God (1 Pet. 2:10). From *laos*, of course, we get the English word *laity*. Laity is a word, therefore, which signifies the elect and holy People of God and distinguishes them from those who are not his people. It is not a word that distinguishes between groups in God's People. Though there are individuals with special functions, apostles, prophets, teachers (1 Cor. 12:28; Rom. 12:6-8), presbyters and overseers (cf. Acts 11:30; 15:2-4; 20:28; 1 Tim.5:1; 4:14; Tit. 1:5-7), none of these functions is a reason for distinction in the one people. It is for this reason that I made the statement that, in the earliest times of the Christian church, there was no such thing as laity as we understand it today.

It is a great peculiarity of Christian history that the word *laos*, which originally meant the entire People of God, has given us the English word *laity*, which now means only a part of that People distinct from another part called *clergy*. In the eyes of many, indeed, laity and clergy alike, not only is laity distinct from clergy, but it is also a less important part of the People than clergy. How that came about will be instructive.

Clergy

In the Jewish tradition, elders (*zeqenim*) provide leadership in the communities. The account in Numbers 11:16-17, repeated in a more general way in Deut.1: 9-18, which reports that Moses appointed seventy elders "to bear the burden of the people with you," formalizes the tradition and validates the leaders as wise bearers of the spirit of Moses and, therefore, of official authority. That this Jewish tradition is continued in the earliest Christian church in Jerusalem is clear from Acts.

Elders are mentioned for the first time, as something not requiring explanation, where they are the recipients of the collection brought from Antioch by Saul and Barnabas (11:30). Later, they again welcome this pair to

Jerusalem to discuss the question of circumcision (15:2-4). They are mentioned again when they gather with James, who clearly presides, to hear Paul's account of his ministry (21:18). Presbyters or elders function as an official authority in both the Jewish and the earliest Christian traditions.

This presbyteral arrangement is not found in the Gentile churches established by Paul. There is no reference to presbyters in any genuinely Pauline letter. This is hardly surprising, for his concept of ministry was controlled, as Congar says it is always controlled, by his concept of church. Paul's church was the Body of Christ, a charismatic Body in which the charismata of the Spirit were given to all, but differently for different ministries (Rom.12:6-8; 1 Cor. 12:4-11; Eph. 4:7-12). All have some ministry to perform in that church.

For Paul, the Spirit had superseded the old Jewish distinction between priest and people and had left it behind. All have ministry in his charismatic church, and any member may be called upon to exercise any ministry for which she or he is gifted. Some have a *regular* ministry, which the community should recognize, encourage and support. "But the idea of mono-ministry or ministerial autocracy—that is, of all the most important gifts concentrated on one man (even an apostle) or in a select group—is one which Paul dismissed with some ridicule (1 Cor.12:14-27)."[80]

The presbyteral arrangement, however, is found again in the deutero-Pauline communities represented in the Pastoral letters, written towards the end of the New Testament era. Presbyters impose hands on Timothy (1 Tim. 4:14). They rule and enjoy special privileges (1 Tim. 5:17-19). They are appointed by Titus in every town to "correct what was defective" (1:5). A presbyter, as seems clear from the evidence, is not just an elder in age, which is all *presbyteros* literally means, but is an elder who has received official office in the people. Timothy and Titus tell us also about another office, that of the *episkopos* or overseer (1 Tim 3:1-7; Tit. 1:6-9).

There is a noticeable difference between the references to presbyters and overseers. Presbyters are mentioned always in the plural, overseers always in the singular, as if there are several presbyters in a community but only one overseer. Spicq relates the still common opinion about the relationship of presbyters and overseer. "The overseer of the pastorals should be considered as a presbyter enjoying here or there a supreme authority, or better a more particularly defined ministry."[81] Presbyter and overseer are synonymous terms, and those who are described by either term belong to the same presbyteral college. But by the time of the Pastoral Letters, where overseer (*episkopos*) occurs always only in the singular, the episcopal presbyter is emerging from the presbyteral college as a *primus inter pares,*[82] a first among equals, functioning as president, guardian, overseer and pastor.

From even this briefest outline of the evidence, it should be clear that there is in the New Testament churches a variety of ministerial structures, from the loosely charismatic structure of prophets and teachers (with very little real distinction between these two) to the more institutionalized presbyteral/episcopal structure. The charismatic arrangement disappeared entirely in the second century or, at best, existed only on the fringes of the catholic church. The institutional structure not only survived, but also became sacralized into a cultic priesthood. It was the development of this priesthood, more specifically the appearance of the notion of *ordo* or order which accompanied it, that gave rise to the notion of clergy (*kleros*) as a class distinguished from, and more distinguished than, laity. When that happened, already by the middle of the third century, the original unity of the people of God had been shattered and was already on its way to being lost. We must, at least, outline how that happened.

In Ignatius of Antioch (d.ca.117), we encounter for the first time a sharply delineated picture of an arrangement in which an *episkopos*-overseer is not just a member of a presbyteral college but also its unchallenged head. His letters to the Magnesians and to the Smyrneans indicate similar ministerial arrangements there, with Damas overseeing the Magnesians and Polycarp the Smyrneans.[83] The overseer presides surrounded by his presbyters, who form his council. "No one is to do anything in the church without the *episkopos*. A valid eucharist is one which is either under his presidency or the presidency of a representative appointed by him. . . . It is not right to baptize without the *episkopos,* nor to celebrate the agape without him. Whatever he approves is approved also by God."[84] The college of presbyters is attuned to its overseer as the strings of a lyre, and conducted by him the whole church sings as a harmonious chorus to the Father through Jesus Christ.[85] The difference between overseer and presbyter, and the preeminence of the former, could not be clearer. But Ignatius still does not ever call the overseer priest, even though it is clear that he alone now ordinarily presides at eucharist.

If Ignatius is the first in the East to present the overseer as more than just a first among equals, Irenaeus is the first in the West. He had been a student of Polycarp, to whom Ignatius wrote as overseer of the Smyrneans, but following study in Rome, he moved to Gaul and became overseer of Lyons about 177. He still uses *presbyteros* and *episkopos*, in their Latin equivalents *presbyterus* and *episcopus,* interchangeably.

Irenaeus urges that it is necessary to obey the presbyters who have succession from the apostles and who, together with this episcopal succession, have received the gift of truth.[87] Because he stands in apostolic succession and hands on apostolic tradition the overseer, of Smyrna or Rome or Lyons, has pre-eminent claim to the title of presbyter, because he stands in a line of presbyters who knew the apostles and who received from them the tradition that is still normative in the church.[88] There is no equivalence between overseers and apostles, for apostles are unique. But overseers are still men of great stature in the community, not because of any special powers they possess, but because they have received the apostolic tradition and the charge to preserve it and because they have been faithful to that charge.[89]

Cyprian, the overseer of the church at Carthage in the middle of the third century, was not as reticent as Irenaeus in maintaining the uniqueness of the apostles. He saw them as the first overseers and the overseers of his day as their direct successors, holding the very same position in their churches as the apostles held in the early communities. This allowed him to argue to the superiority of overseers over other offices in the church, since "the Lord elected apostles, that is, overseers and leaders, whereas deacons were constituted ministers by the apostles."[90]

Cyprian's well-known position on the primacy of the episcopacy, based on its direct connection to the apostles and, therefore, to the Lord, is not difficult to understand. "You should know that the overseer is in the church and the church is in the overseer, and whoever is not with the overseer is not with the church."[91] He argues that the office of overseer is the very foundation on which the church is based, interpreting the Petrine text in Matthew 16:18-19 as applying to it.[92] For all the dignity of the overseer, however, he is elected by the whole Christian community, overseers, presbyters and people alike.[93]

Much more important than his legitimation of the monarchical overseer is Cyprian's casting of Christian ministry into priestly terms. The one chair founded on the rock, which Cyprian interprets to be the overseer, founds not only one church but also one altar and one priesthood,[94] which is to serve that altar and its sacrifices.[95] Because such priesthood is to serve the altar, Priests are to be free from all uncleanness and worldly care and, therefore, like the Levites of the Jewish tradition, are to be supported by the faithful.[96] For Cyprian the *episcopus*-overseer is undoubtedly *sacerdos*-priest. Presbyters share in his priesthood,[97] and Cyprian explicitly delegates them to preside at eucharist[98] and ancient penance[99] in his absence. By sharing in the priesthood of their overseer, presbyters also come to be designated as priests.

From Cyprian onwards, the various roles of members of the people are becoming more and more carefully defined. The first undisputed use of the term *layman* occurs in Clement of Alexandria, at the end of the second century.[100] It occurs in the context of the discussion about the place of sexuality in the Christian movement raised by the Encratites, who taught that all the baptized are called to devote themselves to celibacy. Clement's response to such a position is summarized in this statement. The Apostle Paul "admits that, if his conduct in marriage is beyond reproach, the man of one wife, be he presbyter, deacon or layman, will be saved by begetting children."[101] Only from this moment does the layman emerge from the people of God and, it should be noted, emerge as an elite, that is, one who was of only one wife, as were presbyters and deacons.

It remained for Cyprian to clarify the relationship of this emerging group, *laymen* (the term is correct, for it did not include women), to another group emerging in the church, *clerics.* Their relationship, as we saw above, was articulated in Old Testament terms. The layman was to receive spiritual assistance from the cleric and, so that the latter could be free from the distractions and cares of profane occupations, he was to provide him with financial assistance. This obligation of laymen to provide financial support for the clergy was probably one of the reasons why women, who can be assumed not to have had financial independence, were not included in the term.

When this dual-group arrangement solidified, the transition from the original *laos theou,* the unified people of God, with no distinction of status, to a people of God hierarchically split into clergy and laity was accomplished. We should add here that the transition from an original unpriestly to a priestly ministry was also accomplished. But that I shall explain later.

One way to describe the transition that Christianity underwent in the third century is to say that the original charismatic movement became institutionalized. That institutionalization became ever more fixed when it became legitimate in the Roman Empire with the so-called conversion of Constantine. Though both Cyprian and the earlier Latin theologian, Tertullian, on whom he frequently depends, use Roman political terminology in reference to the church, such use was greatly enhanced when the church was legitimated by and integrated into the empire. I wish to call attention here only to one word and to its meanings.

In the empire, the word *order* (*ordo*) had two principal meanings when used of state officials. First, it designated the highest ranking members of the state, namely, the senators. The term, *ordo senatorius*, order of senators, set that distinguished group apart from the mass of the people. It emphasized rank and dignity above that of the *plebs* or people.

Though there is one disputed text in Tertullian that might be construed along these lines as a distinction between clerics (*ordo*) and laity (*plebs*),[102] Latin theology in general did not adopt this terminology quickly. It is not found in the third-century, Roman *Apostolic Tradition* or in the writings of Cyprian. Secondly, *ordo* referred to any organized group in society, to the order of scribes, for instance, or the order of librarians, or the order of consuls. Jerome speaks in this sense of "five orders in the church: bishops, presbyters, deacons, faithful, catechumens."[103]

In its initial use in the Catholic church, therefore, *ordo* does not refer to inferior or superior ecclesiastical status. It refers simply to ecclesiastical status. To belong to the church at all is to belong to some order. It might be the order of catechumens, or the order of penitents, or the order of widows, or the order of presbyters. But in every case, *ordo* radically expresses the same theological reality, namely, membership in the church whose origin is in Christ and whose final goal is in God.[104]

By the fifth and sixth centuries, however, *ordo* increasingly referred either to the entire body of clerics as distinct from the non-clerical members of the church, or to particular grades within the clerical body: the order of subdeacons, the order of deacons, the order of presbyters, the order of overseers. The stress now is very much on rank, a fact which can be discerned easily from ecclesiastical language. Pope Innocent I speaks of clerics of "both superior and inferior orders,"[105] Leo the Great of clerics of a first, second, third and fourth order.[106]

This clerical use of *ordo* became so much the norm that Gratian was able to assert in the twelfth century, as something taken for granted, that "there are two kinds of Christians," those called clerics, and those called lay. Lay people are allowed to possess temporal goods, to marry, to till the earth, to lay their offerings on the altar,[107] but only as a concession to human weakness. It would be better, he implies, that they not do these things, but since they must it is allowed. This thinking, which is mirrored in other writings of the time, implies the denial that those who have received and who make use of such concessions have any active part in sacred things. That belongs only to clerics. The end result is that not only are there now two groups of Christians, but two quite unequal groups, one following Christ perfectly, the other only imperfectly.

The chasm between these two groups was further widened in the west by two theological developments in the twelfth and thirteenth century churches. The first was that one group was required to live a celibate life and the other was allowed to marry. The second was a change in both the theology and the practice of celebrating eucharist.

In the ancient tradition, the church was known as the true body of Christ (*corpus Christi verum*). In order to be validly ordained to oversee this body, a man had to be appointed to a function in and by this body. In the medieval church the focus of attention switched from church, true body of Christ, to another body of Christ, the eucharist, called the mystical body of Christ (*corpus Christi mysticum*).[108] To be validly ordained to preside over this body, a man needed to be given power over it. This shift of focus in priesthood from pastoral care-church to power-eucharist reached its apogee in the Fourth Lateran Council, which teaches that "no one can accomplish (*conficere*) this sacrament (eucharist) except a priest who has been validly and legitimately ordained."[109] Eucharistic ministry now required not only a man appointed by the church to preside over it, but also a man with the power to accomplish it.

Medieval theology responded to this new focus on eucharist and on the power required for it with a new distinction of power. There was power over a church community (*potestas iurisdictionis*) and power over eucharist (*potestas ordinis*). A man could have the latter without the former; he could celebrate eucharist without any connection to an ecclesial community. He could have priestly power without ever exercising any pastoral ministry in a church. The Council of Chalcedon, whose Canon 6 forbade ordination to the presbyterate without reference to a specific ecclesial community, had made that illegal. But once Chalcedon was superseded, a new church order emerged, one which gave precedence to the community meal rather than to the community whose meal it was. It was but a small step then to the private mass, the celebration of the meal without an ecclesial community present.

The focus on the priestly power of orders as a pre-requisite for celebrating eucharist destroyed another ancient tradition in the church, namely, the tradition of the entire church concelebrating eucharist under the leadership of its overseer-president. An ancient *Liber Pontificalis* teaches that "every age concelebrates," young and old alike.[110] At the end of the eleventh century, Guerricus of Igny teaches that a priest "does not sacrifice by himself, he does not consecrate by himself, but the whole assembly of believers consecrates and sacrifices with him."[111] Congar has shown beyond any doubt that this is the general position of the church of the first millenium: the church communion itself, and not just its *sacerdos-priest* offer the bread and the wine.[112]

That we have to insist on such facts is, of course, a sure sign of how far the church has strayed away, not only from its understanding of itself as the People of God, but also from its understanding that the whole People celebrates as one. Twenty-five years after the Second Vatican Council, which replaced this vision of a church organized by the clergy for the laity by the renewed vision of the church as the People of God, we find that not much has changed.

Laity: A Profile

As already noted, the Council uses the term *laity* "to mean all the faithful except those in holy orders and those in a religious state sanctioned by the church."[113] John Paul II repeats and approves the "positive terms" of this definition, but assigns it as definition of an importantly more specific term, *lay faithful* rather than simply *laity*. The importance of this term becomes apparent when he goes on to explain that "incorporation into Christ through faith and baptism is the source of being a Christian in the mystery of the church."

Christian initiation proclaims and makes explicit and celebrates a person's Christian faith and, therefore, membership in the People of God and in the Body of Christ. *Faith* and baptism, never baptism alone, seal membership in the laity. All believing members of this People and this Body, never baptized non-believers, share in the mission and in the functions of the Christ, who is head of the Body. Each has her and his own function to play in the upbuilding of the church, in accordance with the charisms received and accepted from the Holy Spirit.

The *Code of Canon Law,* published some twenty years after the Constitution on the Church, comes closer to highlighting this notion of a unified people in its definition of "Christ's faithful." They are "those who, since they are incorporated into Christ through baptism, are constituted the people of God . . . They are called, each according to his or her particular condition, to exercise the mission which God entrusted to the church to fulfill in the world."[115] There are still distinctions acknowledged in the people: some are called clerics and some are called lay people.[116] But they are not distinctions between ministers and non-ministers. For, "flowing from their rebirth in Christ, there is a genuine equality of dignity and action among all of Christ's faithful. Because of this equality, they all contribute, each according to his or her own condition and office, to the building up of the Body of Christ."[117]

Paul VI taught that the church "has an authentic secular dimension, inherent to her inner nature and mission, which is deeply rooted in the mystery of the Word incarnate and which is realized in different forms through her members."[118] John Paul II adds to this the explanation that the lay faithful are characterized by a "secular character," which means that the "world" is "the place and the means for the lay faithful to fulfill their Christian vocation." He further insists that this secular character is to be read in a *theological* and not just in a sociological sense. "The term *secular* must be understood in the light of the act of God, the Creator and Redeemer, who has handed over the world to women and men so that they may participate in the work of creation, free creation from the influence of sin and sanctify themselves in marriage or the celibate life, in a family, in a profession and in the various activities of society."[119] A specific characteristic of lay people is that they live in the world where they have "the special obligation to permeate and perfect the temporal order of things with the spirit of the gospel."[120]

The specific vocation of lay people is in the secular world, whereas that of clerics is in the world of the sacred. The intent here is not to suggest that laity have no role in the sacred or that clergy have no role in the secular. It is merely to state what the Popes and the Council take to be obvious, namely, that lay people live and work in the world of everyday reality, that they people the professions and the factories, the schools and the hospitals, the hotels, the fields and the homes. In such ordinary social and familial circumstances, lay people are to incarnate the church and the Christ who is its head, and thereby bring the gospel of reconciliation and salvation directly to the *saeculum*, the world.

The secularity which is a distinctive mark of laity is never to be confused with that secularization of which John Paul II frequently complains.[121] Secularization, on the one hand, is a process in which the material world becomes so dominant, so exclusively "real," that the life of Christian faith is diminished. When that process goes so far as to extinguish Christian faith, then a person has become a *secularized* pagan, a baptized non-believer. Such a person cannot incarnate for the world the church which seeks to minister to it, or the Christ who seeks to bring it the word of God, or the God whose word is reconciliation and salvation. For she or he no longer believes in any of this.

Secular, on the other hand, as it is used of laity, connotes a twofold theological quality of Christian believers. They are, first, firmly located in the secular world and they can, therefore, secondly, incarnate in it the church and the Christ and the God in whom they passionately believe. For a Christian to be secular in this sense is a double badge of honor, for it bespeaks commitment both to the world and to the Christ who is sent to bring it good news and to save it. Such secularity is the distinctive character of the distinctive ministry of lay Christians. It demands great faith, for without faith it easily becomes secularization. But until and unless that sad moment of transformation occurs, Christian secularity should never be confused with pagan secularization.

Without a doubt, secularization always poses a serious threat to lay secularity. But there is another, perhaps greater, and to many certainly less obvious, threat to authentic Christian secularity today. It is a new flight from the world, the flight of laity who, feeling called to ministry, seek out ministries in and to the church rather than ministries in and to the world. Imbued with a new-found sense of ministry, laity in large numbers are seeking to emulate clerical ministries in the *church* rather than to create genuine lay ministries in the *world*.

The problem with this approach does not lie in the fact that laity seek out ministries for which both they and clergy are certainly competent. It lies, rather, in the fact that they flee the very secular ministries for which *only* lay people are truly competent. If lay ministry is ever to become the genuinely secular ministry it can and must be for the salvation of the world, all the People, lay and clerical alike, will need to be on guard against this creeping *clericalization* of Christian ministry.

Pope John Paul II draws attention to two temptations which the lay faithful "have not always known how to avoid." The first is this clericalization of Christian ministry, the temptation to be so strongly interested in church services and tasks that some laity "fail to become actively engaged in their responsibilities in the professional, social, cultural and political world." The second is the constant temptation to separate faith from life, to separate "the gospel's acceptance from the actual living of the gospel in various situations in the world."[122] The Second Vatican Council underscores the double responsibility of priests to "sincerely acknowledge and promote the dignity of the laity and the role which is proper to them in the mission of the church."[123] To be faithful to this responsibility, they will have to promote the Christian secularity of the laity, on which the salvation of the world depends.

Lay Christians themselves appear to have some difficulty with the description of their vocation as secular, and a consideration of this difficulty will help to clarify just what it might mean in practice. In preparation for the 1987 Synod on the Vocation and Mission of the Laity in the Church and the World, the Bishops of the United States entered upon an extensive consultation with laity about their concerns. One of "the most consistent and emphatic" assertions issuing from that consultation was that "church and world should not be divided sharply in our thinking and language."[124] Laity rejected dualism between church and world, between sacred and secular, between even clergy and laity. They rejected any simple equations of the kind church=clergy, world=laity. However much they may be distinguishable in theory, church and world are not separable in fact; nor are sacred and secular, clergy and laity.

The church is incarnate in the world, to be leaven-symbol of love, hope, reconciliation, forgiveness, peace, justice, transformation, grace, presence, mystery. The sacred is similarly embedded in the secular, seeking to become explicit within it and thereby to sanctify it, to transform it from exclusively secular to also sacred, from exclusively people of the world to also People of God, from exclusively bread and wine to also eucharist, from exclusively man from Nazareth to also Son of God. The clergy is part of the laity, the *laos*, the People, seeking to make explicit to the People in proclamation the word of God which calls it to share full responsibility for the church in the world and the sacred in the secular.

There are tell-tale signs, though, of theological schizophrenia. There are signs that what is being rejected is not really dualism but just the designation *secular*. For while laity *say* they are opposed to dualistic thinking, when asked to describe how they connect their Christian life and their secular life, "they speak most often of social services and prayer. There is almost never any mention of actions that involve structural change or include political, legislative or economic strategies."[125] Theologically, or theoretically, laity tend toward a unified view and reject dualistic thinking about church and world. In practice, however, they tend to limit their contributions in the world to recognizably churchy activities, prayer, scripture study, charitable activity, concern for the poor, etc.

The long history of dualistic thinking in the Western church, it would appear, is not supplanted easily, not even in those who are most committed. That fact is neither a great surprise nor a great disaster. It is simply something for the people-church, both laity and clergy, to be aware of, one more concrete manifestation of how long it takes for a communion of disciples to learn what it means for them to be church *in* the world. One more example also, if any more were needed, of the fact that "the church, embracing sinners in her bosom, is at the same time holy and always in need of being purified, and incessantly pursues the path of penance and renewal."[126] It always has to learn that ministry in the church is not all there is to Christian ministry.

Let me illustrate how the ministry of the church in the world works. Several years ago, two faithful Catholics were moved to a new section in the factory in which they worked. It did not take them long to notice that the twenty-two men and women in the section were a very negative group. Their verbal interaction was non-affirming and destructive, the air was blue with foul language and sexual innuendo, the reading material was the latest pornographic epic. My two friends noticed also what a relief it was to everyone when they reached the end of the work day. They heard, too, that the negativity at work spilled over into the home environments. They decided to do something about it.

Dividing the group between them, the two men visited one on one with each person, spending time, listening to personal stories, affirming. Soon the pornography disappeared and the language began to change. The group became more positive and friendships began to form. Finally, after several months, one of the men in the group suggested that maybe they could get together occasionally for breakfast and some prayer. The final outcome was that both work and home became happier places for all the men and women involved.

The beauty of this story of secular ministry is that it is a true story. Two lay faithful, that is, two Christians full of faith, responded to a perceived and dire need in their workplace, and by the simple interaction of love set a group of men and women free from negativity plus. When my two friends started to affirm their colleagues, and when they started to affirm one another, all came alive as individuals and as a group, breathing new life into their relationships both at work and at home. That is what it means to say that the special characteristic of laity is secularity; they contribute to the salvation of the world by ministering in the work-a-day world.

These two baptized believers did ministry by incarnating in the factory the servant church and the Christ who is its head. They had a difficult time understanding that what they did was Christian ministry, every bit as much as what their parish priest did in the ritual of reconciliation was ministry. But it was. Their difficulty in understanding derived from the reverse problem to the one I noted above. In their case theological theory lagged behind ministerial practice. When it was explained to them that ministry was action done in public, on behalf of the church, as a result of a charism of service, proclaimed, made explicit and celebrated in sacrament, to incarnate in symbol the presence of Christ and of the God whose kingdom he reveals, they had no difficulty understanding that what they did was just that.

Let me offer you another, and final, example of ministry in the world. I know a simple man with great teaching ability. He teaches auto body mechanics in a State Technical College, formally initiating young men and women into the mysteries of unbending fenders and rebuilding cars after an accident. Informally, but quite explicitly, he initiates them also into positive self-images (these are not the most favored children in the land), and into justice towards all, accident victims and insurance companies alike. Because of his skill, both as a teacher and as a motivator, he has become quite famous. He now speaks all over the United States and Canada, teaching teachers how to teach students to repair automobiles and egos and injustice.

Across the length and breadth of the continent this man teaches budding auto mechanics not only how to repair automobiles but also how to claim identity as worthwhile people and to deal with all other people in justice. By being his very own sensitive, empathetic Christian self, he serves people with all the talent he has, accommodating his service to the special, secular, needs of the auto body repair shop. He does not have to be convinced, as did the other two, that what he does is Christian ministry. For he sees what he does as action done in public to incarnate the church and the Christ who is its head. He sees it as the genuine ministry of a layperson in the world.

Summary

This chapter sought, ultimately, to do one thing: to challenge the dualism between laity and clergy in the church by recovering the ancient vision of the church as the one, essentially undifferentiated *laos theou,* People of God. This vision, in its turn, inspires another, the vision of an entire church and its each and every member called and designated to ministry. We traced, albeit briefly and in outline, the history of the development of the order of clerics, not to denigrate that development, but to illustrate that it was not always so and, therefore, need not always be so. We drew a profile of laity, emphasizing their essential secularity, to challenge and to inspire all of them to assume their rightful ministerial roles in the church in and to the world. We concluded with two examples of how secular ministry can be done by simple, but ministerially dedicated, Christians.

Questions for Reflection

1. Are you comfortable or uncomfortable with the information that there were no laity and no clergy, as we use the terms today, in the earliest Christian churches? Can you articulate why you feel that way?

2. What does the term *People of God* mean to you? Could there be today, again, do you think, that one People? Do you think that the term *lay* can ever be renewed from its present connotation *less than clergy*? What would be the practical implications of such a renewal?

3. What did you learn from the brief history of the development of clerics (clericalism) in the church? Are you more comfortable with a vision of a lay-centered church or with one of a clergy-centered church? Why?

4. Do you feel drawn to a secular ministry or to an ecclesiastical ministry? What real differences do you see between the two?

5. Do you have any stories to share about the secular ministry of lay women and men?

Suggested Reading

Congar, Yves. *Lay People in the Church: A Study for a Theology* of *Laity* (Westminster: Newman Press, 1959).

Decree on the Apostolate of the Laity, in *The Documents of Vatican II* ed. Walter M. Abbott (New York: Herder and Herder, 1966).

Doohan, Leonard. *The Lay-Centered Church: Theology and Spirituality* (Minneapolis: Winston Press, 1984).

McCaslin, Patrick and Lawler, Michael G. *Sacrament of Service: A Vision of the Permanent Diaconate Today* (New York: Paulist, 1986).

Schillebeeckx, Edward. *Ministry: Leadership in the Community of Jesus Christ* (New York: Crossroad, 1981).

U.S. Bishops' Committee On The Laity, *To Build and Be Church* (Washington: USCC, 1979).

4.

Priesthood:
Ecclesial and Ordained

Ecclesial Priesthood

It is well-known that neither in the New Testament nor in the immediate post-apostolic church is the word *hiereus*, priest, used to designate any Christian minister. John Robinson, as always, states this fact bluntly. "The unpriestly character of early Christianity must surely have been one of the things to strike an outsider, whether he were Jewish or pagan."[127] He proceeds to point out, however, another fact, equally well-known, namely, that "the priestly element in Judaism had not disappeared without trace: it had been transmuted."[128] It had been transmuted to express the roles of Jesus and his church.

The high priesthood of Christ is a central theme of the Letter to the Hebrews (cf. 3:1; 4:14; 6:20; 7:26; 8:1; 9:11). Though not of the priestly tribe, and therefore not a priest "according to a legal requirement regarding bodily descent" (7:16), he is "a priest forever according to the order of Melchisedech" (5:6; 7:1-25). This High Priest is mediator of a new covenant in his own blood (9:15-22; 12:24), and supersedes the Levitical high priesthood and cult. The Levitical high priest entered annually into the Holy of Holies to sprinkle expiatory blood, but this was only a shadow and a type of the action of the great High Priest (9:23-10:1), who "now abolishes the first order to establish the second" (10:9).

There are two points to note here, critical in the history of tradition but frequently ignored. The first is that the presentation of Jesus as the new

High Priest is a presentation not of the entire New Testament, but only of the relatively late Letter to the Hebrews. This letter grew out of questions which troubled the Jewish-Christian communities after the destruction of the temple, and therefore also of the levitical priesthood, in the year seventy. We shall see in a moment how those questions contributed to an extension of Jewish priestly elements even beyond Jesus. The second point to note is that "the epistle to the Hebrews never says that Jesus was *hiereus* in his earthly life: he is high priest now, having entered the Holy of Holies in heaven."[129]

Besides extending the notion of priesthood to Jesus, the New Testament applies priestly characteristics to the church. But just as we must understand that the priesthood assigned to Jesus is not the official Levitical priesthood of his time, but the priesthood of the order of Melchisedech of a much earlier time, so also we must try to understand the priesthood assigned to the church. The first letter of Peter, suffused as it is with priestly talk, is crucial for this question. Chapter 2:4-8 echoes Is. 8:14, Is. 28:16 and Ps. 118:22, passages which speak of a *stone* (*lithos*) which God is laying. Other than the stone there appears to be no common theme. John Elliott, however, draws attention to some Qumran, Targumic and Rabbinic literature which seems to point to a pre-Christian Jewish tradition which combined these texts and applied the *stone* to the Messiah and to the messianic age. "The image had already been prepared; the church simply had to make the application,"[130] an application which sees Jesus as the Messiah and the church as his messianic community. It is in the context of the messianic community that the priestly character of the church is introduced.

The opening phrase of 2:9, "you are a chosen race, a royal priesthood, a holy nation," derives from the covenant formula of Ex. 19:6. This central text expresses the constant theme of Israel's election as the holy people of God. The writer of First Peter uses it to express the election and the call to witness of the new holy people, the church, the living stones paralleled to *the* living stone, the Messiah. For our purposes here only one of the church's characteristics concerns us, namely, its holy priesthood.

In the Hebrew text of Ex. 19:6 there is a parallelism between *kingdom of priests* (*mamleket kohanim*) and *holy people* (*goy qados*). In such Hebrew parallelism the emphasis falls on the second member, in this case the holy people, and the first member is treated as an adjectival clause modifying the second one. The phrase, *kingdom of priests,* therefore, describes the holy people. The people is to be holy as priests are holy, and in this sense it is a *kingdom of priests.* The notion of the elect people is central to this covenant text, and it is this people, not each individual within it, that is both holy and a kingdom of priests. There is no contrast here to the Levitical priesthood, no polemic against it. The contrast is not with the Levitical priesthood, but with "the peoples" (v.5b), that is, the Gentiles. Any interpretation of this text which sees in it an argument against an official priesthood is unsupported by the text, and probably mere *eisegesis.*

That First Peter intends an equally corporate meaning is clear from the corporate designations in v.9: "a chosen race, a kingdom of priests, a holy people, God's own people." Those who are called to believe in the Messiah-stone are themselves living stones built into a Spirit-filled house, a messianic community. It is this community that is a priestly people, not its individual members who are priests.[131] The Book of Revelation makes it clear that it is, ultimately, the heavenly community that is a kingdom of priests (1:6; 5:10; esp. 20:6), indicating the eschatological nature of the priestly people. This notion of the priestly people is still very much to the fore as late as the eleventh century in discussions of eucharistic concelebration. Guerricus of Igny, as we have seen, still teaches then the common opinion that "the priest does not sacrifice by himself, he does not consecrate by himself, but the whole assembly of believers consecrates and sacrifices along with him."[132]

The notion of the church as a priestly community continued in the forefront of the writings of the church Fathers. They link the priestly character to baptism, which is presented as a messianic anointing in image of the anointed Messiah, the Christ, *Christos.* The *Apostolic Constitutions* declares that those who are baptized "are made Christians by Christ, a royal priesthood, a holy people, a church of God; who were once not a people, but now are beloved and elected."[133] Theophilus, Bishop of Antioch at the end of the second century, derives the name *Christian* from our anointing with the oil of God.[134] Augustine teaches that both *Christ* and *Christian* derive from anointing, and that the anointing is to be prophet, to be priest and to be king.[135] Hesychius, fifth century presbyter of Jerusalem, states unequivocally that "the baptized are anointed with a priestly anointing."[136] Jerome is careful to point out that the anointing is not with oil as much as it is with the Holy Spirit.[137]

Ecclesial and Ordained Priesthood

It is generally agreed that priesthood has to do with sacrifice and that sacrifice, as Aquinas notes, has both an internal and an external dimension. The internal dimension, the acknowledgment of total dependence on God, is the essence, and it defines sacrifice. The external dimension, the sacrificial action, signifies the internal, true sacrifice, which is "the first and principal sacrifice."[138] By focusing on these two dimensions, the soul and the body of sacrifice, as Aquinas himself might say, we shall be able to differentiate the priesthood of Christ, the common priesthood of all baptized believers, which I shall call ecclesial priesthood, and the ordained priesthood of some of the church's ministers.

The two dimensions of sacrifice are exemplified well by both the sacrifice and the priesthood of Jesus. The Christian traditions are at one in seeing the death of Jesus on the cross as the once-for-all external sacrifice which reconciled men and women with God. But they are equally at one in acknowledging that the redemptive force on Calvary was not the death of Jesus but the will with which he embraced it. The letter to the Hebrews captures that will.

"Sacrifices and offerings thou hast not desired; in burnt offerings and in sin offerings thou hast taken no pleasure. Then I said, behold I have come *to do thy will*, O God" (10:5-7). Jesus' will from start to finish of his life was sacrificial; he freely and lovingly acknowledged total dependence on God. It is no surprise that such a life should culminate in a death embraced with the same attitude, "not as I will, but as you will" (Matt. 26:39). In an important and well-known passage, the letter to the Philippians expresses the early Christian conviction that the free will of Jesus was central to the redemptive efficacy of his death (2:5-8).

The interior self-giving of Jesus, self-giving not only to God but also to his fellow men and women, made his life the kind of life to which the elect people was called. The death he died expressed that internal self-giving externally, and made it sacrificial. God accepted him in his life and in his death, and by raising him from the dead gave him back to the community of those who believed in him, to be present to them forever as the one who gave and gives himself for them. Jesus exercised the common priesthood of his people in his life and death for others. He continues to exercise that same priesthood, and the priesthood of Melchisedech that grew out of it, now that he has been established by God, through resurrection, as "a priest forever according to the order of Melchisedech" (Heb. 5:6).

We have already noted the election of Israel and the principal effect of that election, the creation of a holy and a priestly people. In Israel, priesthood is first of all a collective quality shared by the entire people of God, and only secondarily an office in which individual members of the people are appointed to mediate for all the rest. The priesthood of the people not only does not preclude the hierarchical priesthood of some individuals, but even leads to it. This is quite in keeping with the Hebrew notion called corporate personality, by which what is given collectively to all is given also individually to one to mediate for all. So it is too in that new elect people called church.

The New Testament calls this People *ekklesia theou*, the gathering called together by God. They have no doubt why God called them together. They are called to believe "that he was buried, that he was raised on the third day in accordance with the scriptures, and that he was shown to Cephas and to the twelve" (1 Cor. 15:4). The new People of God are called to gather in faith, importantly not the faith *of* the historical Jesus but faith *in* the glorified Christ, whom God raised from the dead and made present to his people. The People's function is to incarnate this Christ, that is, to proclaim, to make explicit and to celebrate his transformed presence in the real world of real men and women.

Paul is unshakably clear about this incarnational function. "As many of you as were baptized into Christ have put on Christ. There is neither Jew nor Greek, there is neither slave nor free, there is neither male nor female; for you are all one person in Christ Jesus" (Gal. 3:27-28). In the earliest Christian communities, the incarnational function of the church was summarized in the statement that the church was the Body of Christ (1 Cor. 6:12-20; 10:17; 12:12-27; Rom. 12:4-5; Eph. 1:22-23; 2:14-16; 3:6; 4:4-16; 5:22-30; Col. 1:18,24; 2:19; 3:15). This claim that the church is the real, true and substantial Body of Christ continued for the first one thousand years of Christian history.[139] As already noted, a believer ritually proclaims, makes explicit and celebrates membership in this body in the sacraments of initiation.

The church, then, is the Body of Christ and the elect People of God. It is composed of men and women who have answered God's call to believe in Jesus and in his presence among them, and who have bonded themselves in the ritual of Christian initiation to live in communion with Jesus and with one another. The church, however, is more than just a communion. It is a communion that incarnates the presence of Jesus its Lord in the world; it is a communion that gives a body to the risen Christ as surely as Mary gave the child Jesus a body at Bethlehem; it is a communion that is rightly called, therefore, the Body of Christ. It is a communion that is, as Vatican II taught, "a wondrous sacrament," a sacrament of the unity of humankind in Christ and of the salvation which is offered to everyone in him.[140]

The mission of the sacramental church in the world is a continuation of the mission of Jesus, whom it confesses as Lord and Christ. Like him, it exercises its mission by incarnating in the world, that is by making explicitly present in word and in deed, the Christ and the God who anointed him and sent him to be her servant-minister. The earliest New Testament churches organized this incarnational mission, their ministry, not around the eucharist, however important that may have been to their life, but around the building up of the communion through witnessing to Christ, admonishing to a Christ-like life and leadership toward such a life.[141] The communion itself was prior to its liturgy and, therefore, prior also to its ministers.

For the church to be an effective incarnation of the Christ who is savior and of the God who saves through him, each member of the communion will have to heed Paul's invitation: "Be imitators of me, as I am of Christ." (1 Cor.11:1) Lawrence Olivier once described acting as the actor convincing himself of the role and then, through himself, convincing the audience. So it is with the church and the world. Each member of the church will have to "put on Christ" (Gal.3:27), both his will and his action, and by being and living like Christ convince the world. It is precisely in internal Christ-like will and external Christ-like action that the worship and the sacrifice, and therefore also the corresponding priesthood, of the holy people consists.

The essential sacrifice of Jesus was his internal consciousness of self-giving, to God his Father and to men and women his brothers and sisters. That internal consciousness, a consciousness of being anointed "not to be served but to serve" (Mark 10:45), controlled his external actions, including his death, and made them sacrifice. It cannot be otherwise for the people who claim to be his people. Their sacrifice and their priesthood consist essentially in an internal consciousness of being anointed to serve in the world. They consist materially in the actions of a holy life by which they serve, actions of faith and love and compassion and forgiveness and reconciliation in which they incarnate in the world the presence of the Christ and of his God.

The priesthood and the sacrifice of all members of the church, the elect and holy people of God, belong to the order of a Christ-like life in the world, not to the order of a liturgical life at the altar. "Their work, prayers and apostolic endeavors, their ordinary married and family life, their daily labor, their mental and physical relaxation, if carried out in the Spirit, and even the hardships of life if patiently borne—all of these become spiritual sacrifices acceptable to God through Jesus Christ."[142] All members of the church communion are called to such a holy, sacrificial priesthood.

Each and every member of the lay faithful participates in the mission of Christ as priest (as well as prophet and king), a participation which "finds its source in the anointing of baptism, its further development in confirmation, and its realization and dynamic sustenance in the holy eucharist." Each and every one is called to share in "the priestly mission, for which Jesus offered himself on the cross and continues to be offered in the celebration of the eucharist for the glory of God and the salvation of humanity."[143] It was only when this was forgotten, and priesthood was considered only in relation to liturgical worship, especially to the consecration of eucharist, that people were moved to discount the priestly reality of the church or to subordinate it to the "real priesthood" of hierarchical and liturgical priests. We must now turn to the consideration of this priesthood.

Ordained Priesthood

We have already called attention to the unpriestly character of New Testament ministry. There are many ministries in the New Testament communities, ranging from the Pauline prophets and teachers (1 Cor. 12:28; Rom. 12:6-8) to the *presbyteroi-episkopoi* of the Pastoral letters, but none of them is a priestly ministry. The presbyteral-episcopal structure is the one that *de facto* became dominant, already late in the second century, and ultimately became sacralized into a hierarchical priesthood.[144] This development was entirely legitimate, for the church community can validate the public ministers it needs to be faithful to the Jesus tradition. A little reflection will show that hierarchical priesthood was and continues to be necessary to that faithfulness.

The perennial character of the catholic tradition (which is never to be collapsed into the Roman Catholic tradition) is its wholeness, the seamless relationship between the world, including the human world, and God. The catholic church proclaims, makes explicit and celebrates this wholeness in sacraments. It confesses that Jesus is the visible embodiment or incarnation of the invisible God (cf. Col. 1:15; John 1:18; 2 Cor. 4:4; Heb.1:3). It confesses that it itself is the visible embodiment of the glorified Christ (cf.

1 Cor. 6:12-20; 10:17; 12:12-27; Rom. 12:4-5; Eph. 1:22-23; 2:14-16; 3:6; 4:4-16; 5:22-30; Col 1:18,24; 2:19; 3:15). In contemporary theological language, it has become common to express those confessions by saying that Jesus is the sacrament of God and that the church is the sacrament of Jesus.

As the sacrament of the glorified Jesus, the great High Priest, the church is, as we have seen, essentially priestly. Everything that it is and does is essentially priestly in the sense explained. But as God and Jesus need to be embodied so that bodily men and women can really deal with them, so too the church needs to be embodied so that they can really deal with it. Different *orders* in the church embody its different aspects. Its priestly character is embodied in the ordained priesthood.

As the priesthood of the church itself flows from the priesthood of the glorified Christ and functions for the sake of that Christ, so too does the priesthood of ordained priests flow from the priesthood of the ecclesial community and function for the sake of that community. We have seen already that it took some time for the church to develop both the notion and the reality of hierarchical priesthood. Two other things had to happen first.

First, Christian believers had to think of themselves explicitly as an elect and holy communion quite distinct from Judaism, something that did not happen until after the destruction of the temple in the year seventy and the excommunication of Jewish-Christians from the synagogues in the eighties. Secondly, Christians had to think of themselves in sufficiently sacramental terms to conceive of themselves as offering in some manner the once-for-all sacrifice of Christ. This did not happen, Brown points out, until the end of the first century and the beginning of the second, and it is only then that cultic and priestly analogies begin to be applied to, first, the overseer and, much later, the presbyter.[145]

Priesthood, as we have seen, has to do with sacrifice which, in its turn, has to do, primarily, with an internal consciousness of dependence on and self-giving to God and, secondarily, with external action signifying that internal consciousness. Ordained priesthood flows from and is sacrament of the priesthood of the church. Ordination establishes the priest as a public representative of the priestly church; it establishes him as a vicar of the church (*vicarius ecclesiae*). The very same internal sacrifical disposition that is required of the church that claims to be and to believe in Christ is required also of the church's priest. Absence of this disposition, this faith, this intention to do what the church does, as the unbroken tradition of the church since Augustine teaches, nullifies both his ordination as priest and any specifically priestly act he would attempt.

There has been an endless debate in the church about *how* the eucharist is a sacrifice and about whether it is to be described as a sacrifice of praise[146] or a sacrifice of propitiation.[147] But, from earliest times, there has been an unbroken tradition *that* it is a sacrifice and *that* the principal function of the priest is the concelebration with the church of that sacrifice.

The supreme moment of Christ's exercise of his priesthood was the moment of his death and resurrection. The supreme moment of the church's exercise of its priesthood is the moment of its keeping memory of that once-for-all sacrifice of Christ. The supreme moment of the exercise of ordained priesthood is that very same moment when the ordained priest stands as sacrament of the sacramental church, gathers it together in and as communion to remember the Christ who was sacrificed, and announces to it in prophetic proclamation that Christ is present within it still and forever as the one who gave and gives himself in sacrifice for it.

The Second Vatican Council spoke freely of the People of God. It spoke of it explicitly as the elect people who "by regeneration and the anointing of the Holy Spirit are consecrated into a spiritual house and a holy priesthood." It was at pains to insist, however, that "though they differ from one another in essence and not only in degree, the common priesthood of the faithful and the hierarchical priesthood are nonetheless interrelated. Each of them in its own special way is a participation in the one priesthood of Christ."[148]

It is, of course, one thing to state that the priesthood of the ecclesial community differs in essence from the hierarchical priesthood and quite another thing to clarify what that essential difference is. Pope John Paul II simply repeats without explanation the Council's assertion.[149] The Council itself simply repeats Pius XII's explanation of the difference. "The ministerial priest, by the sacred power he enjoys, molds and rules the priestly people. Acting in the person of Christ, he brings about the eucharistic sacrifice and offers it to God in the name of all the people."[150]

The ordained priesthood is essentially different from the ecclesial priesthood because it is ordained to the ministry of leadership, first the ministry of pastoral leadership and, therefore, also the ministry of liturgical leadership. This reflects the most ancient *Apostolic Tradition* in the church. "Ordination," it reports, "is for the clergy on account of their *liturgical* service."[151]

As I noted earlier, ministry in the New Testament churches is organized around the building up of the community, not around the community's eucharistic liturgy. The common priesthood of all believers is ordained to the worship that is Christian life. The hierarchical priesthood is ordained to that, too, of course, but also to more, namely, to leadership, both pastoral and liturgical. Ordained priests are called to everything to which ecclesial priests are called; they are called also to more, namely, to leadership in the name of the church and, therefore, also in the name of Christ. Both ecclesial and ordained priests are called and appointed to ministry by the Spirit of God and by the church. Ministry, indeed, as Helen Doohan felicitously notes, "is the expression of our spirituality as baptized Christians."[152] But only ordained priests are called and appointed to pastoral and liturgical leadership.

Though both ecclesial and ordained priesthood are participations in the glorified priesthood of Christ, and therefore related one to the other, one is not just a different degree of the other. They are quite distinct in essence because they are quite distinct in public, institutional function and, therefore, community-authorized power. Though there is again some overlapping, they are distinct also in the personal characteristics required for their successful performance. A thumbnail sketch of the personal characteristics that make a good ecclesial priest and that make a good hierarchical priest might help in further distinguishing the two.

Characteristics of an Ecclesial Priest

What sort of person can minister in the world on behalf of the church? The answer would be simple, were it not for a complicated debate on which it touches. There are some who hold that, since a vocation is from God, human charism and talent have nothing to do with it. They forget the ancient Augustinian and catholic tradition: everything created is of grace. If a specific charism-grace of God is required for office in the church, then its presence is a sign of vocation from God and, conversely, its absence a sign of non-vocation. Grace always builds on nature. I stand on this matter, therefore, with a Committee of the New England Catholic Bishops which, while affirming "the divine origin of a vocation," insisted that "such a theology of vocations only increases our obligation to look at many human factors which are observable and which will give us strong hope that a vocation is present."[153]

Richard McBrien has called attention to very general qualities required for ministry and for ministers. These qualities are the virtues required of every Christian: faith, hope, love, prudence, justice, temperance, fortitude, a sound theology, particularly of church.[154] I would like to offer a more specific list, first for the kind of ecclesial priesthood I outlined in the two examples in the previous chapter, and then for ordained priesthood. I shall borrow the characteristics of each from instruments known as the Deacon Perceiver Interview and the Priest Perceiver Interview, and elaborate on them.

Selection Research Incorporated (SRI) of Lincoln, Nebraska, has a long history of success in pinpointing the talents required for occupations varying from executive to secretarial to ministerial. In 1978, SRI developed the Deacon Perceiver Interview, a procedure for detecting the talent/ charism required to be a successful permanent deacon.[155] As such talent/ charism is natural talent enhanced by grace, and since it is either present or absent long before ordination, and is certainly not created by ordination, it must be talent that is present in many Christian men and women who never seek ordained ministry. Indeed, I can say without any hesitation that not only *must it be* present, but also that it *is* present, because via the Perceiver

Interview professional interviewers have documented it in many men and women across the continent who are not seeking ordination. The very same talent that is required for ordained servant ministry may be employed also for non-ordained servant ministry.

Talent/charism for servant ministry is described in three groups of themes, each divided into three sub-themes. There are Core Themes (helping, teaming and accommodating), Motivational Themes (relator, positive others' perception and purpose), and Value Themes (spirituality, family and kinesthetic). I propose to give a thumbnail sketch of each.

The first Core Theme is the *Helping* theme. Persons strong in this theme are sensitive, perceptive, accepting, helping persons, drawn to other persons with needs. They are active in helping others, by attending to the person first and the problem second. The second Core Theme is the *Teaming* theme, which moves people to work at building up a team climate. Teamers are affirming, group enhancing persons, who actively support other team members and enable them to work together effectively and with minimal conflict. The final Core Theme is the *Accommodating* theme, which moves persons to give themselves to others. Accommodators are generous with their time and energy, and they are flexible in responding to the needs of others. They seek affirmation by being of service to others.

The first of the Motivational Themes is the *Relator* theme. Those strong in this theme desire warm, personal, positive relationships with others. They seek to build an atmosphere of trust with others and to get to know them on a personal, supportive level. They enjoy working with others. The second Motivational Theme is called the *Positive Others' Perception* theme. Persons strong in this theme have a history of seeing themselves as self-giving, "good" persons. They want others to see them as good, dependable and helpful. They seek affirmation by relating positively to others, by being helpful to them, by responding to their needs. The final Motivational Theme is the *Purpose* theme. Persons with this theme have a basic belief about the service they do for others; they perceive it as their vocation. They seek servant ministry as a focused way to institutionalize this vocation.

A reader might conclude from what has been said so far about Core Themes and Motivational Themes that a person does not need to be a believing Christian to be a good servant minister. That conclusion would be correct. A person does not have to be a Christian to be a servant. But she or he needs to be a believing Christian to be a *Christian* servant. The Value Themes specify the significant relationships with church, Christ and God that go into the making of such a minister and Minister.

The first of the Value Themes is the *Spirituality* theme. Persons strong in this theme draw upon their sense of church, of Christ and of God to specify and to fuel their vocation to be of service. They take seriously Christ's command to "love your neighbor as yourself" (Matt. 19:39), and they seek to respond to that command in the service of the church to which they really feel they belong. Their deep faith in God, in his Christ and in his church gives them the confidence and the strength to be of service over the long and difficult haul. They exemplify Doohan's insight, cited earlier, that ministry is the expression of the spirituality of baptized Christians. The second value theme is the *Family* theme. Persons strong in this theme place a high priority on family. They have had strong family ties all through their life, and such ties continue in adulthood, whether they be married or single. They integrate family into everything in their lives, into their jobs as well as their ministry. All the other themes are linked together by the final Value Theme, the *Kinesthetic* theme, which describes persons of high energy levels, always on the go. Those who have this theme like to be active, have a great deal of stamina, and see their activity as a service contribution to others. Their purpose and spirituality themes focus their energy.

Those who possess all these themes in greater or lesser measure will make more or less outstanding servant-ministers. All over North America, suitable candidates to be ordained deacons are being sought out through the application of the Deacon Perceiver Interview. I do not wish to dwell on that here, however. I wish only to call attention to the fact that such talent/charism abounds in the People of God, that it can be perceived by trained observers, and that it needs to be called to be of service in the up-building of the People into the Body of Christ.

The greatest source of stress and burnout in ministry, as in many professions, derives from the mismatch between the work to be done and the worker appointed to do it. The Perceiver themes remove this source of stress by matching work and worker, ministry and minister. It would be naive to suggest that ministers who score highly in all of the themes will experience no stress in their ministry. But it is in no way naive to suggest that they can avoid burnout by dealing sensitively and sensibly with the normal stress of their helping, purposeful, kinesthetic lives.

Characteristics of an Ordained Priest

SRI has produced also a Priest Perceiver Interview, which uncovers the talent/charism required for the successful performance of ordained priesthood. A look at the ordained priest themes will enable us to contrast them with those of the ecclesial priest and help us, perhaps, to understand better the essential difference between the two. I shall divide the fourteen themes that define an outstanding priest into three sub-divisions, Core or Can-Do Themes, Motivational or Will-Do Themes and Action or How-Will-Do Themes.

The first Core theme is the *Presence* theme, which defines people who are regularly and spontaneously conscious of the presence and beneficent action of God in their lives and in the lives of others. This consciousness produces a constant response to the present God and a constant desire to lead others to experience her presence in their lives. This Presence theme may be *the* critical Core theme for the ordained priest. Those with this theme have sensed God's presence and action in their lives from a very early age, and they have responded to it so persistently that they may not ever be aware of a particular time in life when they were called to the priesthood. The Presence theme functions at its best when it is allied to the next theme, the Relator.

The *Relator* theme designates persons who desire positive personal relationships with others and who can devise strategies to build such relationships. Positive relationships cover the spectrum from a minimum of acceptance of others as human beings to the maximum of a willingness to give one's life for others. The priest-relator moves easily beyond the minimum to seek extended and enduring relationships of mutual support with others. From the strictly human point of view, it is hard to imagine any genuine priestly effectiveness if both the Presence and the Relator themes are not merely present, but also strong.

The *Enabler* theme is the third Core theme. It indicates the experience of satisfaction a person derives from noting each increment of growth in another person. The enabler is attuned to noticing growth, to appreciating and affirming growth and to making further growth possible. Enabling priests free people for growth by teaching them, by delegating responsiblity to them and by supporting them in their efforts to use their responsibility for the building up of the Body. They take every opportunity to assist people to understand the meaning of their experience and to identify their options. When they make decisions, the enabling priest respects their need to take ownership of their decisions and supports them in their struggle to do so, thereby making success and further growth possible for them.

Then there is the *Empathy* theme. Empathy is the capacity for reading the feelings of others and for feeling with them. It is a powerful theme, which may be used not only to develop a trusting relationship with others but also to manipulate them. Other themes determine just how empathy will be used, but effective priests use it to sense and to articulate the feelings of others and their readiness to disclose and deal with them.

The final Core theme is *Courage*, defined in this case as the capacity for asking others to make commitments. Courageous priests are able to voice important and relevant ideas, directly and straightforwardly. They are able to take charge and to give directions when necessary. Resistance strengthens their resolve, but does not make them angry at either the obtuseness or the matching resolve of others. The empathetic and courageous priest is ready to meet with people at very difficult times in their lives, to feel with them and for them, to call attention to their talents and to point out to them their opportunities for Christian growth.

When a person possesses all the Core Themes, that is, when she or he can-do priesthood, there still remains a question: "Will that person do priesthood?" Without other themes, Motivational or Will-Do themes, the answer is open, maybe yes, maybe no. There are five Motivational Themes. The first of them is the *Mission* theme. This theme moves people out of the mainstream of a society to take the lead in preserving its quality and its resolve to be faithful to its founding reason for existence. Those who possess this theme perceive in every task a significance that far transcends the task itself. By consistently giving expression to this transcendent meaning, priests aid people in seeing the meaning and purpose of their lives, both human and Christian. For priests, mission is entirely other-centered; they spend their lives for the development of others, especially for their spiritual development.

A powerful Motivational theme is *Hope.* Priests possessing this theme view the future, including the ultimate future, with great optimism. They help people create visions for both their own future and the church's future, nourish these visions and generate assurance that the God who renewed Jesus from death can renew and fulfill the deepest human desires.

Closely allied to the theme of hope is the theme of *Loyalty* to the Catholic Church. Loyal priests commit and dedicate themselves to the church, identifying with its history and its tradition as others might identify with a family or a nation. Their identification is forever. Even in times of great difficulty for the church, even in times that appear to be a betrayal of the church, the loyal priest sees the historic tradition and the hopeful future along with the diminished present.

Then there is the *Community* theme. This theme leads priests to build and maintain belonging and fellowship and interaction among members of their community. Those with this theme enhance the way people feel about their community and their part in it, and they are particularly sensitive to what those who belong want the community to be and to become. Through their stimulation, the church communion becomes a support system for all its members.

The final Motivational theme is *Ego Awareness*. If the ego drive is one that impels a person to define herself or himself as significant, then ego awareness is the capacity to identify the events, the achievements, the affirmations, the feelings, that led to the liberating self-assessment: I am significant. Those with high ego awareness can be very explicit about such self significance. Though they may not like all of their thoughts or actions or feelings, ego aware priests can own them and, when appropriate, disclose them. Those with high ego awareness are most likely to be, and to be perceived as, more objective and, as a result, more trustworthy. Those with low ego awareness are very likely to deny their own thoughts and feelings that depart from the required norm. As a result, they are likely to deny or to misunderstand the feelings of others, and so come to be mistrusted by them.

If people possess the Core themes and the Motivational themes, if they both can and will do priesthood, only one question remains. How will they do it? Four Action themes provide the answer to that question. The first is the *Focus* theme, which designates the capacity to take a direction and to maintain it. Those with focus are able not only to identify goals, actively pursue them and not be diverted from them, but also to help others to do the same. A sense of focus projects a sense of continuity and security. Priests with focus are able to set priorities and then select strategies to achieve these priorities in order of importance. Those who lack focus project a sense of energy-diffusion. They start many projects but finish few, creating in themselves a sense of dissatisfaction and of insecurity.

Focus is greatly aided by the *Arranger* theme, which names a capacity for organizing persons, things and settings to yield a desired result. The effective arranger is a stage director, with the ability to anticipate and facilitate group interaction. Priests are called constantly to be arrangers, both of liturgical worship and of endless church meetings. The arranger-priest establishes carefully crafted settings, liturgical and otherwise, that put people at ease and enable them to experience freedom, personal choice and tolerance for ambiguity.

A crucial priest theme is *Omni*. This theme characterizes a person who believes in completeness and in answers, who looks for completeness and for answers, but who also can accept and live with the incomplete and the unanswered. Such a person is stimulated by mystery, loves to formulate hypotheses about mystery, is sometimes perplexed by mystery, and is always comfortable with mystery. This theme goes beyond the mere toleration of ambiguity to the positive enjoyment of dealing with ambiguity and of clarifying it. The stark need for this theme in one who is ordained to represent and to deal with Mystery is obvious. "For many, burnout means a disparity between expectations and achievement. There is a nagging sense of incompleteness and a lack of fulfillment."[156] Not in priests with Omni. They may not always be able to offer absolute answers, but they are able always to affirm that answers are there to be discovered, and that they are best discovered together.

The final theme is the *Conceptual* theme. Priests with this theme can articulate for themselves and for others the meanings of their human experiences, the meanings of the catholic tradition and the points of convergence between the two. They are both fluent and powerful in their verbal ability. They are also constant learners, ever ready to reflect on their experiences and to reflect back what the tradition has to say to such experience. They can speak the word of God in and to human experience. They are, in traditional religious language, powerful prophets.

Even this summary consideration of ministerial themes should help to clarify both the points of convergence and the points of divergence between ecclesial and ordained priests. The convergence occurs in the general ecclesial fact of the many and different talents/charisms gifted by the Spirit of God in Christian initiation, including "the participation of the lay faithful in the threefold mission of Christ as priest, prophet and king."[157] The divergence occurs in the specific fact of the difference of charisms, the ecclesial priest being talented as a servant-helper, the ordained priest being talented as a servant-leader. For the convergence to be of value to the mission of the church, to underscore something to which we have already alluded, ordained priests "ought to acknowledge and foster the ministries, the offices and the roles of the lay faithful that find their foundation in the sacraments of baptism and confirmation, indeed, for a good many of them, in the sacrament of matrimony."[158]

The Perceiver Themes confirm the ancient theological tradition, namely, that the difference between the ecclesial priest and the ordained priest is a difference of talent/charism, those competent to carry out the functions of ordained priesthood being essentially gifted with the charism of leadership. This gift of leadership fits them for the presidency of the communion (pastoral leadership) and, therefore, also for the presidency of the eucharist (liturgical leadership) in which the communion proclaims, makes explicit and celebrates its special character as communion and as the Body of Christ.[159] The earliest traditions indicate that it was a person who was fitted for the former who assumed also the latter. To avoid being misunderstood, however, in my claim that the ecclesial priest is essentially a helper and the ordained priest essentially a leader, I need to specify and to clarify it by making two concluding points.

The first is an analogy, derived from a well-known educational setting, the local school. In that school, there are many teachers but only one principal. Each teacher has charge of a particular class and of all that goes on in that class. She is the leader of that class, but only of that class. The principal, on the other hand, is the leader of the entire school. She is charged with enabling, not just the students but also the teachers. She must build community among all of them and generate loyalty to that community. She must have the conceptual skill to articulate an educational vision for the school and the courage to hold herself, the teachers and the students to it. She is the overarching leader of the school. In relation to her, the teachers, who are undoubtedly leaders in their own classes, are helpers. So it is also with ordained and ecclesial priests.

Priest-bishops in their dioceses and priest-presbyters in their parishes are the overarching leaders charged with the building-up of the entire communion. In that overall context ecclesial priests, who are certainly leaders in their own individual ministries, are their helpers, building up specific parts of the communion into the whole through their specific ministries. Here, however, I must insist on a caveat. The analogy I have offered is never to be understood as in the halcyon days of Catholic Action, when bishops and priests monopolized ministry and shared *their* ministry with lay helpers. In contemporary theology, only the church monopolizes ministry and shares that ministry with both ecclesial and ordained priests on the basis of their different baptismal charisms. My analogy suggests only that, within the overall context of church ministry, the ministries of ordained and ecclesial priests are related as leadership and helping ministries.

The second, and utterly critical, point is this. If the ordained priest is to be an ecclesial leader, and if the charism of leadership can be detected by trained observers, then it behoves the church community to seek out such leaders to ordain. For the charism of pastoral leadership, not ritual ordination, defines the essential status and authority of a priest in the People of God. In ordination, the community does no more than acknowledge the already-present talent/charism of pastoral leadership and endow it with sacramental power. If such leadership were uncovered and nurtured before ordination and then brought forward for ordination, the rite of ordination would be in very deed a proclamation, a making explicit and a celebration of leadership. It would be a ritual in very truth acknowledging a pastoral leader and endowing him also with sacramental or symbolic power.

The alternative, frequently practiced in and rendered doubtful by history, is to use the ritual to attempt to endow with sacramental power a person who may or may not have the talent/charism of leadership. That alternative, a modern variation on the absolute ordination proscribed by the Council of Chalcedon, is too great a risk for the church to take in the crisis which presently, and indeed always, threatens it. For if the fit between pastoral leadership and sacramental power turns out to be a misfit, then only disaster awaits both for the priest who is not a leader and for the community which would then be leaderless. The response to the question of the ordaining bishop, "Do you judge him to be worthy?," if it is to be meaningful and helpful to the church, ought always to include the statement, "This communion judges him to be a pastoral leader."

One final comment about the themes of both ecclesial and ordained priests will conclude this chapter. Henri Nouwen summarizes the meaning of all Christian ministry in the Lord's saying: "A man can have no greater love than to lay down his life for his friends" (John 15:13). "If teaching, preaching, individual pastoral care, and celebrating are acts of service that go beyond the level of professional expertise, it is precisely because in these acts the minister is asked to lay down his (or her) life for his friends."[160] Professional competence of whatever kind is never anything more than a preparation for Christian ministry. Ministry does not occur until the minister brings to it not just his or her competence, but also his or her very self.

Teaching becomes ministry only when ministers offer not just the knowledge they possess, but also themselves. Preaching becomes ministry only when ministers tell not only the generalities of the Jesus story, but also the specifics of how the story affects them. Pastoral care becomes ministry only when ministers offer not only professional and mechanical competence, but also themselves in all their non-competent weakness and woundedness as a source of creative healing. Celebrating becomes ministry only when celebrants move beyond the safety of prescribed ritual to unite each man and woman in their communion with the Mystery which embraces all, not only in ritual but always and everywhere.

The difference between mere professional competence and creative Christian ministry is provided by ministers who offer not just competence but also themselves. Both ecclesial and ordained priests who possess the themes outlined above are outstandingly equipped to do just that. That is why the church needs to reinforce their evident call to service from the Holy Spirit of God with a more discerning call of its own.

Summary

This chapter dealt with priesthood in the church, the priesthood of Jesus, the priesthood of his church and the priesthood of the church's ordained priests. It dealt with all of these priesthoods in terms of sacrifice in general and in terms of the sacrifice of Jesus in particular. Sacrifice consists essentially in an interior will of total dependence on God, ritualized in external action attuned to that will. The sacrificial will of Jesus the priest was externalized in his actions of self-giving to God and to others, culminating in his self-giving on the cross. The sacrificial will of the priestly People is externalized in the self-giving actions of a Christ-like life in the world. The sacrificial will of the People's ordained priests is externalized specifically in their offering on behalf of the People the sacrificial meal[161] which keeps memory of the once-for-all sacrifice of Jesus. The chapter concluded by detailing themes that characterize both ecclesial and ordained priests, and by challenging each to engage in the helping and leadership ministries for which they are respectively gifted and, therefore, called.

Questions for Reflection

1. How do you react to the information that no minister among the many recorded in the New Testament is called *priest*? If there were no priests in the earliest Christian churches, how do you think the communities managed?

2. What does it mean to say that the church is a *priestly People*? How does it manifest itself as such?

3. What do you understand by the term *sacrifice*? What essential sacrifice is involved in the daily life of Christians? How does that sacrifice measure up beside the sacrifice of Jesus on Calvary and the sacrifice offered by the ordained priest in eucharist?

4. The chapter argued that ecclesial priesthood is essentially a helping priesthood and that ordained priesthood is essentially a leadership priesthood. How do you understand the sameness and the difference between the two?

5. Please consider the qualities of an ecclesial priest and of an ordained priest as detailed in this chapter, and rate yourself honestly against them. Do you think you would make a good priest? (Many people, for the sake of a false humility, are tempted to rate themselves low. Please try to be as honest as you can and to avoid such false humility.)

Suggested Reading

Brown, Raymond E. *Priest and Bishop: Biblical Reflections* (New York: Paulist, 1970).

Doohan, Helen. *The Minister of God: Effective and Fulfilled* (New York: Alba House, 1986).

Fenhagen James C. *Mutual Ministry: New Vitality for the Local Church* (New York: Harper and Row, 1986).

McBrien, Richard. *Ministry: A Theological, Pastoral Handbook* (San Francisco: Harper and Row, 1987).

Power, David N. *Gifts That Differ: Lay Ministries Established and Unestablished* (New York: Pueblo, 1980).

5.

Ordained Priesthood
in the Church

The Tradition

By the sixteenth century, the theology and practice of ordained priesthood in the western church had solidified in the direction of a priesthood empowered to consecrate and to preside at eucharist. That theology and practice, which was not supported in all respects by the theology and practice of the New Testament and the apostolic church, both eastern and western, was further solidified and validated by the Council of Trent in the sixteenth century.

Like all historical gatherings, the Council of Trent met in a specific historical setting. Two factors are important for understanding the teachings of the Council within this setting. The first is well-known: the Council wished to highlight only those Catholic truths which had been challenged by the Reformers. It explained, for instance, at the beginning of its document on the sacrament of orders, that its doctrine was "the true and Catholic doctrine *to condemn the errors of our time.*"[162] It is to be understood, therefore, only in this context. It is not a complete setting forth of even the Roman Catholic doctrine of orders, and still less a complete setting forth of the catholic doctrine, but simply an affirmation and validation of only those facets denied by the Reformers.

The chapter on orders concludes, therefore, with the clearest of statements. "These are the things which it has seemed good to this sacred Council to teach the faithful *generally* about the sacrament of orders."[163]

Generally, not *specifically*; a partial teaching, not all that could be, or needs to be, said. That there was, and still is, much more to be said has been clear since Trent. For the very polemical circumstances of the time led the Council to respond generally in a very one-sided cultic way, which ignored the valid, and New Testament-rooted, non-cultic aspects of ministry in the Christian churches.

A second historical factor in the setting of the Council of Trent is as well-known as the first, but is more frequently forgotten and/or ignored. That fact is that there was a complete absence of any representation or influence from the eastern catholic churches, an influence which would have provided a balance to what Trent was willing to teach about orders and ministry in the *catholic* church. For all intents and purposes, Trent was a synod of the *western* or Roman Catholic church, not an ecumenical Council of the *catholic* church.

Whatever be the answer, however, to the question of whether or not Trent was an ecumenical Council, one thing is beyond dispute. The teachings of the Council on the sacrament of orders were narrow teachings, which did not reflect either those points of agreement between the Reformers and the Catholic tradition or even the much more extended theology of orders dealt with by the Council in its three sessions. The Bishop of Avignon complained at the time that "the proposed doctrine is in no way pleasing to me because it does not embrace the whole reality of this sacrament, as it promised in its preface and as it ought to do to confirm the truth of the Catholic faith and to stamp out the heresies which have arisen in our times about this sacrament."[164]

Four propositions drawn from the teachings of the Reformers were presented to the Bologna session of the Council in 1547. The first stated that orders is not a sacrament, but only an office; the second that it is a power to preach, not to offer; the third that all Christians are equally priests; the fourth that bishops have no power to ordain and that ordinations they perform are invalid. Four years later, at its session at Trent, other propositions were added: in the New Testament, there is no such thing as a visible priesthood; there is no such power as the power to consecrate the body and the blood of the Lord or to forgive sins; there is only the office to preach the gospel and whoever does not preach the gospel is not a priest; there is no such thing as hierarchy. Even a cursory glance at the teachings of the Council of Trent on orders will reveal that all it did was defend the ordained ministry that had developed in the western tradition and present it as church order.

The Tridentine canons leave no doubt about the position of the Roman church with respect to ministry and priesthood in the sixteenth century. There is a visible priesthood in the New Testament. There is a power to consecrate the body and the blood of the Lord, and to forgive sins. There is a power to do more than simply preach.[165] The canons do not say, but the corresponding chapter does, that these powers are located in the ordained priesthood.

It was the understanding of Trent's teaching in later history that hardened the Roman church's understanding of ministry as exclusively priestly and cultic, so that ministry came to be understood as something that priests did, certainly not lay people. Against the overall history of the catholic church, such a view is a diminution, not only of ministry, but also of priesthood. I do not agree, however, with the suggestion that the Council of Trent invented this view, for there is abundant evidence to show that it was an established view long before the Council.

The polemical context in which the Council met and produced its teaching tended to obscure one simple fact, namely, the Reformers were not simply wrong in everything they said. They were not wrong, for instance, in advancing preaching as a central New Testament ministry and office. They were wrong only in claiming that it was the only office and ministry blessed in the New Testament. But in the Catholic counter-reformation so much emphasis was placed on the cultic duties of priests that the impression was given that cult was all there was for a priest to do. The medieval *potestas ordinis* appeared more and more as a *potestas cultus,* a fact which is easy to discern from even a cursory reading of Roman statements about priesthood from Trent to the present day.[166]

The Council of Trent, in Ganoczy's words, was "a more or less valid and effective reply to Lutheran and Calvinist questions and challenges.

But [history] has also recognized that in the course of the following four centuries a too rigid desire to stick to the letter of the Council has sometimes blocked the progress which ought to have taken place within the structures of the church, in response to new challenges and questions."[167] Trent produced no systematic ecclesiology. But its insistence on the essentially hierarchical nature of ministry produced in the four centuries following it a matching insistence on the essentially hierarchical nature of church.

Church was imaged, not as the one New Testament People of God, but as a pyramid of institutional power, at the apex of which ruled the Pope assisted by the hierarchy and at the base of which knelt an obedient People.[168] That model of church, and of ministry, dominated the ecclesiology of the Roman Catholic church until the Second Vatican Council, which attempted to supplant it with a communal model more in tune with the ancient tradition of the broad catholic, as distinct from the narrowly Roman Catholic, tradition.

The Tridentine model of church and ministry, Tridentine only in the sense that it derived inevitably from Tridentine principles, was constructed on the notion of the power wielded by one segment of the church over the other segment. Vatican II attempted to renew that model by restoring an older model in which power was shared in the one People, both laity and clergy, and in which their union as disciples of a common Lord was emphasized over their distinction of function. Twenty-five years later the jury is still out on how successful that attempt has been.

The Reformers, as we have seen, taught that orders was only a power to preach in the church and not a power to consecrate and offer gifts. In 1546, Trent prepared a disciplinary decree *Super Lectione et Praedicatione,* which taught that the principal task of a bishop was to preach the gospel, a task he was to carry out at every opportunity.[169] Unfortunately, it did not proceed with this decree, and in fact withdrew from it lest it appear too "Protestant". Vatican II had no such qualms.

The Council taught explicitly of bishops that, among their principal tasks, "the preaching of the gospel occupies an eminent place."[170] It taught of priests that "in the image of Christ the eternal high priest, they are consecrated to preach the gospel, shepherd the faithful and celebrate divine worship."[172] They have "as their primary duty the proclamation of the gospel of God to all."[173] The power of the priest over eucharist is still to the fore. But Trent's desire to declare preaching of the word a primary task of the church's ordained ministers, four hundred years and endless polemics later, finally came to fruition.[174]

Vatican II's Priest

It is probably a sign of the complacency of the times that there was no document on priests among the documents prepared for discussion at the Second Vatican Council. One can only suppose that it was assumed that the nature and the role of the priest had become sufficiently well established and elaborated to need no further treatment. That was certainly the assumption for many theological realities in the days of the preparatory commissions.

What little the Council was supposed to say of priests was located in a short section of the Constitution on the Church. When that document was being discussed, however, at the second session in the Fall of 1963, there were numerous complaints that what was being said of priests, on whom the church so depended for leadership, was too skeletal and an equal number of demands that it be fleshed out in a fuller treatment. The document that was finally approved in December, 1965, *Presbyterorum Ordinis,* offered a broadened vision of priesthood.

No longer is the priest viewed simply as the cultic man. Rather is he seen, first, as a member of the People of God, a disciple of the Lord, a brother among brothers (sic!). He is seen, secondly, as a man set apart from, but not separate from, his people to shepherd them into communion with one another and with their common Lord. He is seen, of course, as unquestionably male, as the questions we shall raise in the next chapter had not yet begun to be seriously aired for discussion. An outline, however skeletal, of this priest will be helpful.

It is a fact of great theological significance to the church that when the Council opened its discussion of ordained priesthood, it drew attention first to the common priesthood of all believers. The ministerial church comes before its ministers and its ecclesial ministers come before its ordained ministers.[175] Ordained priesthood emerges from the ecclesial priesthood common to all believers; the nature of ordained priesthood emerges from a consideration of the common mission of the church and of all its members.

But all the members of the church do not have the same function in it, and the Lord "established certain ministers among the faithful in order to join them together in one body."[176] These ministers are, of course, the priests of whom this document speaks. Their ministry is "not confined to the care of the faithful as individuals, but is also properly extended to the formation of a *genuine* Christian community."[177] The *pastoral* leadership and care of the community, which I so emphasized in the preceding chapter, is confirmed by the church in Council to be *the* talent/charism of the ordained priest. It behoves all priests, ecclesial and ordained alike, to ponder carefully the communion-church which they are called to lead.

The sacred scriptures, the record of the self-understanding of both Judaism and Christianity, are quite clear on the communal nature of both religions. God's revelation of himself begins with the election of a holy people, united in their faith that God led them out of Egypt and into a land flowing with milk and honey. From that people emerges yet another holy people, united in their faith that the God of Abraham and Isaac and Jacob raised Jesus from the dead and called them to be the People of that risen Lord. The New Testament underscores the communion-forming action of that Lord in the images of the church as the Body (1 Cor. 12:12-27), as the Vine (John 15:1-8) and as the holy People of God (1 Pet. 2:9).

The bond that binds the People together is not so much something they share in common, their faith in Jesus, for instance, as it is their common bond with him, who is present forever to them as the one done to death and raised by God to glory. Much of the activity of the early communion is done for the building up of the Body (Eph. 4:12; cf. 1 Cor. 14:12; 2 Cor. 10:8; 13:10), but that does not mean that it is turned only inward. All are instructed to "do good to all," even if "especially to those who are of the household of the faith" (Gal. 6:10).

The Council's teaching makes the priest specifically responsible for the contemporary building up of the Body. It makes him responsible also to gather together a communion that looks, not only inward to itself, but also outward to the bigger world. Its Pastoral Constitution on the Church in the Modern World, *Gaudium et Spes,* is its clearest articulation of how that task is to be done.

Priestly ministry, as explained by Vatican II, embraces a twofold minis- try, a ministry of the word and a ministry of sanctification.[178] "Since no one can be saved who has not first believed, priests, as co-workers with their bishops, have as their primary duty the preaching of the gospel of God to all."[179] No longer is the preaching of the word suspected to be a "Protestant" activity; it is the primary duty of presbyters, both bishops and priests. It is by preaching the word that they both follow the Lord's com- mand to "go into the whole world and preach the gospel to every creature" (Mark 16:15) and build up the Body of Christ.

But lest the notion of the word that is to be preached be too narrowly in- terpreted, the Council makes clear that it is a twofold word, contained not only in sacred scripture but also in the celebration of eucharist. "The faith- ful receive nourishment from the twofold table of sacred scripture and the eucharist."[180] It is from these two tables that priests are to nourish their flock; their proclamation is to be not only in word but also in deed. Thus they are to build up the communion and the Body of Christ.

Both proclamations are sacred, for both are drawn from a sacred source and directed to a sacred goal. Each is, therefore, to be Spirit-filled and self-filled, always reflecting not just mechanical but also, and primarily, personal understanding and competence. Priests, therefore, drawing on all the resources of the church and personal traditions, are to study the twofold word assiduously, to make every effort to understand and integrate it before it is spoken. For only when it is integrated can it be proclaimed to hearers convincingly.

This task of preaching the word is not to be conceived solely in the ordinary meaning of preaching. Priests fulfill their task of preaching "whether they engage people in conversation and draw them to glorify God, or openly proclaim the mystery of Christ to non-believers, or catechize believers and explain the doctrine of the church to them, or comment on the questions of the time in the light of the mystery of Christ."[181] Reflection on the questions of the time in the light of the word of God is what the tradition calls prophecy. Such prophecy has ancient precedent and legitimation in the church, though it long since was absorbed into the hierarchical ministry. Priests are invited to be prophets again, that is, to speak the word of God in contemporary situations. But, since prophecy is not exclusively the charism or the task of ordained priests, they will have to learn again to listen to lay prophets and to nurture them. For prophecy is to build up the body of Christ. It may not be good for comfort levels, but it is good ecclesiology.

If priests are to proclaim God's word, not just in some abstract fashion but in concrete circumstances, then they need to be as conversant as they can with those circumstances. Since they must preach the gospel to men and women and children of varying levels of education and development and condition, they must cultivate the art of relating to all. They must "learn especially the art of speaking to others in a suitable manner, of listening and communicating patiently and with reverence imbued with love, so that the mystery of Christ living in his church can be made known."[182] Such pre-evangelization is necessary, not so that priests can be numbered among the guys, but so that the word of God they are called to preach can be preached as efficiently as possible. To truly know their sheep, shepherds must live in the sheepfold.

Long before the special option for the poor became common currency, the bishops of Vatican II had proclaimed publicly that the poor and the lower classes were to be a special concern for bishops[183] and for priests.[184] It cannot be otherwise in a community that claims to believe in and to be the body of the Christ who was united to the poor (Matt. 25:34-45) and for whom the proclamation of God's word to the poor was an authentic sign of messianic activity (Luke 4:18). Indeed, the commitment of the church and, therefore, of its priest-leaders, to the poor cannot truly be called an *option*, as if it were something that they could take or leave. It is an option only in the sense that it is a choice that it makes. But it is also a choice that it *must* make if it wishes to claim to be the sacrament in the world of him who was sent "to preach good news to the poor . . . to set at liberty those who are oppressed" (Luke 4:18).

There remains that other word that is very specifically entrusted to ordained priests. Priests have not ceased to be persons of the cult, they have ceased only to be exclusively that. The eucharist remains both the source and the apex of their proclamation of the word. It is "the summit toward which the activity of the church is directed; at the same time it is the fountain from which all her power flows." It is the very heartbeat of the believing communion.[185] That should not come as a surprise to the church.

In the eucharistic concelebration, the People with their leader keep memory of Jesus who was raised from the dead by God, who was made both Lord and Christ (Acts 2:36), who is forever present in their communion, but never more explicitly than when they gather to eat and drink in his memory. Every one of the church's priests, both those of the ecclesial priesthood and those of the ordained priesthood, concelebrate that presence and, precisely by concelebrating it, make it explicitly real, true and substantial presence. But it is the ordained priest whose public ecclesial function it is, acting on behalf of the church and therefore also of Christ, to consecrate and offer gifts.

It is his liturgical function that essentially distinguishes the ordained priest from the ecclesial priest. It is in this function, above all others, that ordained priests share in Christ's ministry "of unceasingly building up the church on earth into the People of God, the Body of Christ and the Temple of the Holy Spirit."[186] It is in eucharist that they, and all who make up Christ's Body, can proclaim in thanksgiving (*eucharistia*) and praise (*exomologesis*)[187] their foundational and ambivalent word: "This is my Body."

I wish to mention one final element that Vatican II adds to the sketch of the ordained priest. It is an element long ago noted in Augustine's famous dictum: "For you I am a bishop, but with you I am a Christian."[188] The Council borrows this idea and paraphrases Augustine's language. Priests are priests and fathers "in Christ Jesus through the gospel" (1 Cor. 4:15). But they are also "brothers among brothers with all those who have been reborn at the baptismal font. They are members of one and the same Body of Christ, whose upbuilding is entrusted to all."[189]

Ordination into the order of ordained priesthood does not nullify prior membership in the People of God; it does not nullify the priesthood shared in common with all. Ordained priests, both priest-presbyters and priest-bishops, remain radically members of the People, the *laos*. Though the church continues to define laity in distinction from clergy, it enjoins upon all priests to "sincerely acknowledge and promote the dignity of the laity and the role which is proper to them in the mission of the church."[190]

The use of the two verbs, acknowledge and promote, indicates, I believe, a twofold task. Ordained priests, first of all, have to acknowledge the dignity of lay people as members of the People of God and of Christ's Body, and they have to realize that dignity is one they share with them. Given the burden of a significantly different history, that acknowledgement and understanding might not come easily. Twenty-five years after Vatican II, many lay people are coming to believe that it has not happened at all. But happen it must before both priests and laity will be free to carry out together their respective tasks in the building up the Body. Because that building up is both a common goal and a common duty, priests are, secondly, to promote the dignity of lay people.

There are many lay people, probably a majority, who need to hear John Paul II's resounding words. "The lay faithful are given the ability and the responsibility to accept the gospel in faith and to proclaim it in word and deed."[191] There are many who still conceive the church and ministry in hierarchical categories, in the worst possible meaning of that term, conceiving church and ministry in dualistic terms, clergy and laity, them and us, ministers and non-ministers. There are many who still say of church and hierarchy it is "their church," and "their job to run it."

Ordained priests have the duty to call such people, as did the United States Catholic Bishops, to Christian adulthood, holiness, ministry and service in the church and world.[192] It is only when the true identity of the layperson in the church is understood and accepted by both the laity and the clergy that both will be able to work as one people for the building up of the church, the one People of God, the communion with and in Christ and the sacrament of Christ in the world.

Paradoxically, the true Christian dignity of both laity and clergy will be promoted best by abolishing both terms, at least as terms that separate. Only when all the faithful share their common dignity as members of the one People of God, only when each values the others and communion with them, will each be totally free to perform his or her ministerial function for the building up of all into the Body of Christ. Only when all, lay and cleric together, proclaim with one voice "This is my Body," will that proclamation be any way true and effective.

Ordination as Sacrament

What does it mean that ordination is a sacrament? The answer to that question depends on the definition one assigns to sacrament, a definition that has varied through the centuries.[193] I have already defined sacrament as a prophetic symbol which proclaims, makes explicit and celebrates the presence and action of grace. The question at issue in general always is: what grace is proclaimed, made explicit and celebrated in this sacrament? The question at issue specifically here is: what grace is proclaimed, made explicit and celebrated in the sacrament of ordination? An initial answer can be derived from a traditional way of speaking of ordained priests. They are vicars of Christ (*vicarii Christi*), even other Christs.

The phrase *vicarius Christi* appears first in Tertullian, though he referred it to the Holy Spirit.[194] Later in the third century, Cyprian, his fellow North African, applies the image, if not the exact phrase, to the bishop, who acts in the place of Christ (*in vice Christi*).[195] Presbyters were spoken of in the same way as early as the end of the fourth century,[196] and thereafter it became a commonly accepted way of speaking of both bishops and priests in the catholic churches.

In papal documents of the modern era, this view of the priest's role is dominant, and it is presented in a eucharistic context and in function of the power of orders. Priests are the "Redeemer's legates"; they take the place of God (*Dei vices gerit*); they take the place of Christ (*Personam gerit Domini nostri Jesu Christi*).[197] Vatican II echoes this view, teaching that in the celebration of eucharist the priest acts in the name of Christ, "brings about the eucharistic sacrifice, and offers it to God in the name of all the people." The people, for their part, "join in the offering of the eucharist by virtue of their royal priesthood."[198]

It is one thing, though, to state that a priest is a vicar of Christ and acts in the person of Christ, and quite another thing to ground that assertion theologically. The traditional grounding, itself grounded in a Scholastic theology which links sacraments directly to Christ without any mediation on the part of the church, has been to deal with vicar of Christ as a function of the power of orders. In this approach, the representative function of priests derives from institutional considerations. By the mere fact that they have been ordained to the apostolic office of presiding at eucharist by one who himself holds the apostolic office of overseeing the church, and who stands in an unbroken line of succession going back to the apostles and, indeed, to Christ himself, priests are vicars of Christ.

This traditional insistence on an almost physical succession of ordination going back to the apostles and to Jesus himself has served to institutionalize and objectify the representative function of ordained priests. But it is open to several objections. First, the unbroken succession which it supposes is historically more than doubtful. Secondly, it too unilaterally ignores the mediation of the church communion in the process of ordination, putting too much weight on the sacrament as a source of power over the eucharistic body of Christ and no weight whatever on the pastoral power required to preside over the ecclesial Body of Christ. Thirdly, it totally ignores the fact that the presence of Christ in sacrament is not just an objective presence, but also and, more properly, a personal presence, and therefore has as much to do with personal disposition as with sacramental power.

Objective presence is always drawn into personal presence only by personal faith. Edward Kilmartin, speaking of eucharist, states that "without the exercise of faith no sacramental presence of Christ or the passion of Christ is possible."[199] He is correct, I believe, when he goes on to insist that considerations of the role and of the importance of personal faith "are germane to the question of the representative role of apostolic office. They point to the conclusion that office directly represents the faith of the church and only to this extent can represent Christ."

In what sense is orders sacramental and what does it sacramentalize? It is sacramental in the sense that it proclaims, makes explicit and celebrates the church as faithful and God and his Christ as the source and guarantor of that faith. The *and* can be and has been misleading, however, especially when it is read disjunctively. I need, therefore, to rephrase to underscore what I intend. Ordination is a sacrament in the church in which believers (I do not say *male* believers) are designated as representatives of Christ in so far as, and to the extent that, they are faithful representatives of the faithful church. I must explain this assertion.

The Second Vatican Council speaks of several modes of Christ's presence in the church. He is present "especially in liturgical celebrations"; he is present in eucharist, "not only in the presence of his minister . . . but especially under the eucharistic species"; he is present in the sacraments "by his power"; he is present in the proclaimed word; he is present in the praying church.[200] The preparatory schema had sought to establish an order in those presences, from Christ's abiding presence in the church to his presence in word, prayer, sacrament and eucharist. That effort could not win enough votes in the assembly and the theologically weaker text cited above was agreed on. The stumbling block to the ordering effort was the desire of the majority of bishops to give precedence to Christ's presence in the eucharistic minister (*vicarius Christi*) and in the eucharistic species (*corpus Christi*).

When God, the almighty Father, raised Jesus from the dead, he established for all time his objective, glorified presence in and for the world. But, to be real presence objective presence needs to be drawn into personal presence. Though I am objectively present in a football crowd, it cannot be said that for most of the crowd I am personally present. For most of them, indeed, I am not really present at all but really absent. So it was and is with the post-resurrection presence of Jesus. It needed and needs to be drawn from mere objective presence into personal, and therefore humanly real, presence.

The objective presence of the risen Christ was drawn into real presence initially by the faith of the first believers, who believed in the mighty work of God in raising Jesus from the dead and making him manifest as the Christ. It was this faith, ongoingly interpreted, that became the faith of the church, the apostolic faith preserved in the catholic church and shared with each local church. Apostolic office is an office of witnessing to and pastoring in and into that apostolic faith in the name of the church.

Priestly ordination establishes believers directly in an office and a ministry of service to the faith of the church; it establishes them as representatives of the church, vicars of the church. It is only to the extent that they are ordained as representative vicars of the church that they are ordained also as vicars of Christ, who is mysteriously one with the church. Ordination establishes believers in an order of ministers who act directly in the name of the church, and only indirectly in the name of Christ.

There is, as Congar has noted, "a Christian mystery which embraces Christ and his ecclesial body."[201] Because of the union between Christ and his church, a union so important that the church images it in that most unique of human unions in marriage,[202] what is done in the church as vicar of Christ is done and can be done only and to the extent that it is done as vicar of the church. We have traced, admittedly briefly, because the facts are well-known and not disputed, the development from the New Testament ideas of the one High Priest, the priestly People and non-priestly ministries to the priestly ministries of the third century. That development leads to the inescapable conclusion that there developed in the church, undoubtedly under the prompting of the Spirit of God (John 16:13), a presbyteral ministry of witnessing to faith in the glorified Christ and of overseeing other ministries aimed at building up the Body of Christ. That ministry is today the ministry of the ordained priest.

It is because they have the talents/charisms required for pastoral leadership in the church (*potestas iurisdictionis*), the ecclesial Body of Christ, that the church endows priests also with sacramental power (*potestas ordinis*) over eucharist, the sacramental Body of Christ.   Ordination proclaims, makes explicit and celebrates, that is, the double presidency of priests, their power to act as vicars of the church and, therefore, also as vicars of Christ. This approach to presbyteral leadership in the church is clear as far back as the *Apostolic Tradition*, where we find it expressed in the consecration of both bishops and priests.

The prayer for the consecration of a bishop prays the Father, who knows all hearts, to grant him "to feed your holy flock, to exercise sovereign priesthood without reproach, to make known incessantly your propitious face, to offer the gifts of your holy church." That for the consecration of a priest prays for him to "help and govern your people with a pure heart."[203] To the extent that the expression vicar of Christ is appropriate at all, it appears "linked, not to the power to consecrate, but to the charge to build up and to preside over the church."[204]

The catholic principle of wholeness is at work here again. Ordination establishes believers as representative sacraments of the church united in apostolic faith. This church, in its turn, is sacrament of the Christ, the source and the object of faith. In his turn, this Christ is the sacrament of the great God-Father who raised him from the dead and showed him to Peter and to the Twelve and to James and to Paul (1 Cor. 15:5-8).

Ordination, like every other sacrament in the church, is a sacrament because it proclaims, makes explicit and celebrates gracious reality far beyond the literal reality of the words and actions which comprise it. Ordinary words and actions proclaim, make explicit and celebrate in a believer the faith of the apostolic church, which ordains him or her in those words and actions to be its representative and, because its representative, representative also of the Christ whom it confesses as its Lord. The words and the actions of the ordination ceremony seek to make clear that the election-ordination is the work not only of the church, but also of the Holy Spirit of God.

What, then, happens in the sacrament of ordination? The ordaining bishop, representative leader of the local church to the great Catholic Church and of the Catholic Church to the local church, lays hands on each individual to be ordained and prays over them the prayer of consecration. For priests he prays: "Almighty Father, grant to these servants of yours the dignity of the priesthood. Renew within them the Spirit of holiness. As co-workers with the order of bishops may they be faithful to the ministry that they receive from you, Lord God, and be to others a model of right conduct."[205]

The words and the gestures of the ritual are meaningful on several levels. They symbolize: 1) the election, by the apostolic church and, therefore, also by the Spirit of God, of a believer who shares the faith of the church (absence of this faith nullifies the sacrament); 2) the public verification of the apostolic faith of this believer by the one who has the office of guaranteeing the faith of the local church, its bishop; 3) the ordination of this believer to an office of pastoral leadership in the church,[206] an office in which she/he is a *vicarius ecclesiae*, that is, a designated representative of the church, both local and Catholic; 4) the ordination, therefore, of this believer as also a *vicarius Christi*, an other Christ, so that when she/he proclaims the gospel, forgives sins, or blesses bread and wine, it is the church and the Christ who proclaim, forgive or bless; 5) the authoritative proclamation of the presence in this believer of the talent/charism of leadership and of the Spirit who is the source of all charisms, and the celebration of this Spirit to strengthen her/him for the pastoral task of "building up the community through preaching, admonition and leadership";[207] 6) the separation of this believer from the church, to stand over against it both to represent and to animate its faith, a separation which is to be understood as maintaining rather than severing connection, much as Christ the head is both separated from and connected to the church which is his body.[208]

The election of believers, the verification of their faith, their ordination, the proclamation of the Spirit and his gifts in them, their separation from the church, all are to be regarded as permanent and need not, and therefore cannot, be repeated. The permanence of all these elements constitutes the character which Catholic theology has traditionally assigned to the reception of this sacrament.

Ordination establishes the priest in a *holy order,* but the meaning of that phrase needs careful attention. It can be clarified by reflecting back on what I said earlier about order, namely, that to belong to the church at all, as catechumen, penitent, believer, deacon, presbyter or bishop, is to belong to a holy order. The talent/charism of pastoral leadership, which is initially gifted by the Holy Spirit to a believer in baptism, is proclaimed, made explicit and celebrated in another sacrament, the sacrament of ordination, in and through which the believer is established in a new order in the church. It is a *holy* order, not because the ordained alone are holy, still less because they are holier than other orders in the People, but simply because it is an order in the People all called to holiness.[209] "Holy order is, in the first instance, neither an office nor a function, but a quality manifested by the entire church when its behavior imitates the Lord's, when its teaching is faithful to the apostle's message, and when its leaders are trusted exemplars worthy of imitation by all."[210]

The restored recognition of Christian initiation as the ritual source which proclaims, makes explicit and celebrates the ministerial gifts of the Spirit[211] should not and does not preclude the need for further sacramental order in the church. For the charism of leadership is always authorized in ritual, both inside and outside the church. And that is exactly what happens in ordination. The talent/charism of pastoral leadership possessed by a believer is proclaimed and made explicit for all to celebrate, and is further enhanced with sacramental authorization.

Because of the presence of the Spirit of God and his gifts of apostolic faith and pastoral leadership in them, believers are ordained to priestly ministry in the church. They are ordained, that is, to action in public, on behalf of the church, as a result of the charism of servant leadership, to incarnate in symbol the presence of the Christ and of the God whose kingdom he reveals. Those initially ordained to Christian ministry in the sacraments of Christian initiation are now ordained anew and specifically to the Christian ministry of pastoral and liturgical leadership. They are ordained, not to monopolize but to promote and challenge all ministries through their own ministry of exemplary leadership. It is thus that they are to build up the Body of Christ which is also the People of God.

Summary

This chapter sought to situate and to deal with ordained priesthood within the perspective of the model of church as the People of God. Therefore, it related ordained priesthood and the common ecclesial priesthood of the People, and specified it as a task and a function of leadership in the People. It sought to show how ordination establishes priests as both pastoral leaders of the church-Body of Christ and liturgical leaders of the eucharist-Body of Christ. While the sacraments of initiation establish all believers as members of the People, the sacrament of ordination designates some of them as representative leaders of the People (*vicarii ecclesiae*). Only to the extent that they are first members and designated leaders of the People are priests members and representatives of Christ (*vicarii Christi*). Only because they are first members of the holy order of the People of God are they then members of the holy order of the clergy. This chapter sought to renew both holy orders, so that the People generally and the clergy specifically might be challenged to see their original holy unity as the indispensable source of their subsequent and secondary differentiation.

Questions for Reflection

1. When the Second Vatican Council wanted to speak of ordained priests, it spoke first of the common ecclesial priesthood of all believers. Why do you think it did so? What implications do you see in the strategy?

2. How do you understand the terms *holy orders of the Christian People* and *holy orders of the clergy*? Are they any way meaningful to you? Do they carry any obligations?

3. What is the relationship between pastoral leadership and liturgical leadership in the church? What do you believe happens in the sacraments of Christian initiation and of ordination? What are the implications for Christian living?

4. What do you understand by the term vicar of Christ? What are the practical implications for priests and for the People?

5. What is your personal vision of priesthood in the church? How does your vision of priesthood fit into your vision of church?

Suggested Reading

Audet, Jean Paul. *Structures of Christian Priesthood: A Study of Home, Marriage and Celibacy in the Pastoral Service of the Church* (New York: Macmillan, 1968).

Decree on the Ministry and Life of Priests, in *The Documents of Vatican II* ed. Walter M. Abbott (New York: Herder, 1966).

Galot, Jean. *Theology of the Priesthood* (San Francisco: St. Ignatius Press, 1984).

Kilmartin, Edward. *Church, Eucharist and Priesthood* (New York: Paulist, 1981).

Lawler, Michael G. *Symbol and Sacrament: A Contemporary Sacramental Theology* (New York: Paulist, 1987).

Mitchell, Nathan. *Mission and Ministry* (Wilmington: Glazier, 1982).

Osborne, Kenan B. *Priesthood: A History of the Ordained Ministry in the Roman Catholic Church* (New York: Paulist, 1988).

Schelkle, Karl H. *Discipleship and Priesthood* (New York; Herder and Herder, 1965).

Schillebeeckx, Edward. *The Church with a Human Face: A New and Expanded Theology of Ministry* (New York: Crossroad, 1985).

6.

Women in Ministry

Preamble

Readers of the preceding chapter may have been struck by the careful use of non-gender pronouns throughout. They may also have been surprised, for they may legitimately have expected male pronouns in a chapter dealing with ordained priesthood. It is well-known that the Roman Catholic Church has never admitted women to the ordained priesthood and that, in recent years, it has iterated and reiterated its intention not to abandon that tradition.[212]

I am well aware of those facts and, as a Roman Catholic theologian, I acknowledge them with respect. But, precisely as a theologian in the People of God, I feel impelled to state calmly that those facts do not definitively settle the questions about women and ministry raised today in the People. Our age is not the first to raise such questions,[213] but it is the first to raise them in a context in which the equal dignity of male and female Christians is assumed by so many theologians. That assumption leaves neither the questions nor their context the same.

The question of women in the church's ministries has become more and more focused in the past twenty years, as women have tried to translate into church practice the gains they have made both in ecclesial theology and in secular society. Though it clearly included them in every discussion and statement about the role of laity in the church, the Second Vatican Council made few explicit statements about women. But one of them, added only in the final drafting of the Decree on the Apostolate of the

Laity, asserted explicitly that "since in our times women have an ever more active share in the whole life of society, it is very important that they participate more widely also in the various fields of the church's apostolate."[214]

Twenty years after the Council, the final document of the 1985 Extraordinary Synod moved in that same direction. It asked the church to "do its utmost so that (women) might be able to express, in the service of the church, their own gifts and to play a greater part in the various fields of the church's apostolate." It asked pastors to "gratefully accept and promote the collaboration of women in ecclesial ministry."[215] The 1987 Synod on the Laity repeated that plea, after noting the debt of gratitude owed by the churches to those faithful lay men and women who have collaborated unselfishly with the clergy and religious to build up the church to the ends of the earth. It urged bishops, priests and deacons to "receive and accept the gifts of the Spirit in the lay faithful," including women, and to "stimulate the sense of communion and responsibility." It affirmed explicitly again the human dignity of women, which is equal in every way to the dignity of man. "The People of God is made up of the baptized, in equal dignity and common mission, each with his or her particular vocation and task."[216]

It has to be admitted, though, that such ongoing talk has produced in practice little that responds to the concerns of many dedicated women in the church. This fact has led one spokeswoman to state that "if you're a woman, there is very little in the Catholic world that is new for women. Except talk of course. . . . There is indeed a lot of talk, but unfortunately very little else is actually done."[217] I have no wish merely to add to the talk, not as a theologian and certainly not as a male. But I am in total agreement with Canadian Archbishop Chiasson, who said at the conclusion of the 1987 Synod that "when religious leaders feel they have the Holy Spirit and others do not, they are afraid of dialogue. But the day you believe the Holy Spirit is working in other people in the world, you are not afraid to open the dialogue."[218]

I agree with Chiasson also in believing that the Holy Spirit is furiously at work in the church today, in women as in men, in unordained as in ordained ministers. What is needed is not continuing platitudes about things that have already been said better elsewhere, nor the secrecy of silence that Chiasson said marked the Synod. For what do we have to hide from those with whom we are in communion? What is needed today, as it has always been needed, is communal discernment of spirits (1 John 4:1). In this chapter, as a small contribution to that process of discernment, I shall focus the analysis of the previous chapters on three separate, but not unrelated, questions. They are questions about women and ecclesial ministry, women and non-ordained institutional ministries in the church and women and ordained ministries in the church.

Women and Ecclesial Ministry

This ought to be a very short section, for the question it raises is easily answerable by anyone who knows the theology of Christian initiation. For the sake of clarity and for future reference, I shall set out that theology in the form of a Scholastic syllogism. The communion of Spirit-gifted women and men with and in Christ, the church, the People of God, is born in faith and in baptism (Can. 204). But baptism proclaims, makes explicit and celebrates "a genuine equality of dignity and action among all of Christ's faithful," an equality which enables all to "contribute, each according to his or her own condition and office, to the building up of the Body of Christ" (Can. 208). Therefore, all of Christ's faithful, that is, women and men alike, enjoy an equality of dignity and action for the building up of the Body of Christ and of the People of God. As equal members of the essentially ministerial church, all are called to use their gifts in ecclesial ministry to make effective the mission of the church.[219]

If the premises of the foregoing syllogism are correct, and as a Catholic theologian I accept them as correct from the magisterium of the church,[220] it proves that, though they are different, women and men are equal in Christian dignity and action. That women are different needs no proof in a patriarchal church. But that they are equal most certainly does. That being so, I will forego my initial intuition that this ought to be a very short section to dwell on the equality of Christian men and women in a little more depth.

After its affirmation, cited above, of the "human dignity of women, which is equal in every way to the dignity of man," the 1987 Synod tersely cited Genesis. "Man and woman he created them" (1:27). It was not the best or the clearest text to cite to show the equality of man and woman, at least not when left unexplained. For the biblical scholarship of the last twenty-five years is percolating only slowly into Catholic culture, and understanding of the first chapters of Genesis continues to be skewed. They continue to be read, not as a testimony to the equality of men and women before God, but as a testimony to their essential *in*equality. A more extended analysis is, therefore, required.

I do not wish to launch here an extended treatment of biblical theology. That is already readily available in hundreds of good introductory textbooks. But I do need to ensure that readers understand the Catholic biblical tradition so that they can understand what follows. I will take as my starting point for a summary of that tradition a recent statement of the Bishops of the United States on biblical fundamentalism.[221]

According to this statement, "biblical fundamentalists are those who present the Bible, God's inspired word, as the only necessary source for teaching about Christ and Christian living." For them, the Bible alone, totally free from any religious, historical or scientific error, *sola scriptura* in the most naked sense, is all that is necessary. The Catholic tradition holds otherwise. While it too acknowledges that the Bible is God's word to humankind, it acknowledges also that it is comprised of "a collection of books written under divine inspiration by many human beings." To reach the religious truth that God wishes to communicate through it, therefore, requires careful study and interpretation under the guidance of a living communion that seeks that truth across the centuries. That living communion is, of course, the church.

The study that is required to attain biblical truth embraces the study of the ancient languages in which the various books are written, as well as the patterns of thinking and writing and interacting of the people who wrote and initially read them. It embraces also, as Vatican Council II taught, close attention to the literary forms in the books. "For truth is proposed and expressed in a variety of ways, depending on whether a text is history of one kind or another, or whether its form is that of prophecy, poetry, or some other kind of speech. The interpreter must investigate what meaning the sacred writer intended to express and actually expressed in particular circumstances as he used contemporary literary forms in accordance with the circumstances of his own time and culture."[222]

It is important, the United States Bishops teach, that every Catholic "realize that the church produced the New Testament, not vice versa." Dunn puts this point succinctly. The evidence of all the evangelists and Paul "is that each community of the Spirit and each new generation of the Spirit felt the responsibility to interpret the received tradition afresh and in relation to its own situation and needs."[223] There never was a time when there was any kerygma other than the one interpreted and proclaimed by the church, not so much about the historical Jesus as about the risen and glorified Christ. The church came first, the New Testament second. So it was, too, with the Old Testament. The People came first, and only then the records of their interpretations of the great covenant events. Which brings us back to the book of Genesis, a composite of diverse records.

The God *Yahweh* presented in Genesis is unlike the gods worshipped by the peoples surrounding Israel, for she has no cooperation in the act of creation. She needs no cooperation, for Yahweh creates by her word alone. The zenith of her creation, the Hebrew creation account tells us, is *'adam*, male and female. "Male and female she created them and she named them *'adam*" (Gen.5:2). And this is where an understanding of the language and of the patterns of speaking and writing of that ancient people comes in. For "she named *them 'adam*," that is, man and woman together, not a man called Adam and certainly not a woman called Eve. Yahweh named man and woman together *'adam*, earthling, humankind.

That fact alone, that man and woman *together* are *'adam*, founds their radical equality as human beings, whatever different roles and functions later history and culture and hopelessly erroneous biology will assign to them.[224] It establishes them as "bone of bone and flesh of flesh" (Gen.2:23), as "ribs" (2:21) and enables them "therefore" (that is, precisely because they are equal) to marry and to become "one body" (2:24). The Bishops of the United States cite with evident approval the judgment of

Pope Paul VI. "God created the human person—man and woman both—as part of a unified divine plan and in his own image. Men and women are, therefore, equals before God: equal as persons, equal as children of God; equal in dignity and equal in rights."[225]

It is because there is no similar shared equality between 'adam and the animals, because indeed 'adam lords it over them (he/she "gave names to . . . every beast of the field" Gen. 2:20), that there is found no "helper fit for him" (2:20). Because of that radical inequality, no companion fit for 'adam, male or female, can ever be found among the animals. Bestiality is forever forbidden to both him and her.

The radical equality of man and woman before God was heavily obscured by the patriarchal societies in which both Judaism and early Christianity flourished. For the relationship between man and woman taken for granted, then as now, in those Mediterranean societies inevitably became a factor in the interpretation of biblical texts. At the outset of this book, I stated that the discussion would be informed by the model of church as community of disciples. Elisabeth Schussler Fiorenza has argued convincingly that the earliest Christian churches were not only communities of disciples, but also communities of equal disciples.

All four gospels present women as the primary witnesses for the fundamental events of early Christian faith. "They were eyewitnesses of Jesus' ministry, suffering and death and burial. They were first told the easter message and then sent to the male disciples to proclaim the resurrection."[226] Modern biblical scholars argue that, in a cultural setting in which the equal priority of women with men could not have been imagined or invented, these facts about women could have been universally reported only because they were true. The earliest Christian community must have been, indeed, a discipleship of equals and, therefore, a counter-cultural movement in the patriarchal societies in which it came into being.

Fiorenza extends the *human* equality of man and woman into their *Christian* equality, their equality in Christ and in his People, the church. She does this on the basis of the baptismal text in Galatians 3:28: "There is neither Jew nor Greek, there is neither slave nor free, there is neither male nor female; for you are all one person in Christ Jesus." The meaning of this text is, of course, hotly debated, especially as the equality it so clearly asserts is disputed by the so-called household code of Colossians 3:18-4:1. That debate cannot be reproduced here. I wish only to state that I am in agreement with Fiorenza's conclusion. "Paul's interpretation and adaptation of the baptismal declaration of Gal. 3:28 in his letters to the community of Corinth unequivocally affirm the equality and charismatic giftedness of women and men in the Christian community. Women as well as men are prophets and leaders of worship in the Christian community."[227] That, indeed, women as well as men were leaders in the early Christian movement is now well-acknowledged. But I shall reserve a treatment of that fact until the next section.

There is another household code in the Letter to the Ephesians 5:21-6:9. It opens with a strange injunction: "Be subject to one another out of reverence for Christ" (5:21). The Greek word that the Revised Standard Version renders as reverence is *phobos*, fear, the kind of fear that the Old Testament declares to be the beginning of wisdom (Proverbs 1:5; 9:10; 15:33; Ps.111:10). This fear is a radical awe when confronted by the mighty works of God.

The letter writer takes over the household code from traditional material, but in 5:21 he critiques it, challenging the absolute authority of any one Christian group over any other. When faced with the mighty work of God that raised Jesus from the dead and called into being a church of equal disciples, Christian women and men stand in awe and give way to one another, contrary to the established cultural codes. The inequality between man and woman and between the roles assigned to them in a patriarchal society is essentially overcome through baptism, which creates between them a renewed equality that manifests itself in counter-culture social behavior.[228]

The contradiction between Paul's reporting of both that equality and the traditional Mediterranean inequality is more apparent than real. For when he "fought those who defended the old—his bold vision of the new expressed itself most strongly as in Gal.3:28. When he discerned the overstatement of the new, he spoke up for the old."[229] In a community of equal disciples, of course, it is quite ludicrous to have to spend time demonstrating the equality in Christ of men and women. Many commentators wonder if the fact that it has to be done so extensively today is a sign that the Christian churches have been socialized more by the patriarchal societies in which they originated than by the Jesus movement to which they profess allegiance. Whatever be the answer to that question, the answer to the originating question of this section should now be self-evident. Can women be ecclesial ministers in the communion that is the church of Jesus? Of course they can and, in fact, always have been. So let us move on.

Women and Non-Ordained Ministries

The Second Vatican Council's vision of the church as a community of equal believers, as should be clear by now, opened up new perspectives, not only of church but also of ministry. It led to calls for restructuring, to bring the practice of ministry in the church into line with renewed theology. On August 15, 1972, Pope Paul VI issued two documents, *motu proprio,* that is, under only his own signature, which inaugurated that restructuring. They were *Ministeria Quaedam*, which dealt with minor orders, and *Ad Pascendum*, which dealt with the restoration of the permanent diaconate.[230] Though the latter is an important sign of changed ministerial theory and practice in the church, only the former concerns us here.

In *Ministeria Quaedam*, Pope Paul suppressed the minor orders of exorcist and porter and the application of the word *order* for the ministries of lector and acolyte. Though the latter are retained as ministries in the church, they are no longer to be reserved to clerics or to be considered as conferring any special status on those who receive them. Drawing inspiration from Vatican II, in the success of which he played such a significant part, the Pope explained that the church desires that all the faithful take a full and active part in liturgical celebrations. For "such participation by the Christian people as 'a chosen race, a royal priesthood, a purchased people,' is their right and duty by reason of their baptism."[231]

The ministries of lector and acolyte, therefore, may now be exercised by the baptized in virtue of their share in the priesthood of Christ. But because of their liturgical importance, they are to be exercized by those who have been both chosen and designated publicly through a special installation. Reneging on the implied equality of men and women derived from baptism, but in keeping with the "venerable tradition," the Pope restricts these ministries to men.

The real import of *Ministeria Quaedam* does not lie in its opening the ministries of acolyte and lector to the lay faithful, nor in its restricting them to men. As David Power correctly observes, its real contribution lies in the extent to which it helped "focus our attention on the truly vast, complex and rich reality of lay mission and ministry in the church."[232] For, besides establishing the Ministries of lector and acolyte, Paul VI also urged that "there is nothing to prevent episcopal conferences from requesting others of the Apostolic See, if they judge their institution to be necessary or very useful in their region."[233]

In *Ministeria Quaedam* Pope Paul specifically mentioned the ministries of porter, exorcist, catechist and the works of charity. In a later exhortation, *Evangelii Nuntiandi*, he added "directors of prayer and chant, Christians dedicated to the preaching of God's word or the familial service of their brethren in need, the heads of small communities, the leaders of apostolic movements, and such like."[234] Many lay, non-ordained ministries are possible in the church. The only real question is: can any of them be exercised by women? Or, when will the church acknowledge again the venerable tradition of the discipleship of equals?

Though many episcopal conferences responded to the invitation to institute official lay ministries, one can serve as a representative exemplar for all. In 1975, the church in Brazil issued a report on the exercise of official lay ministries in that country. Among those ministries they listed minister-president of the Sunday assembly, minister of the eucharist, minister of baptism, minister of funeral rites.[235] Later there was added official minister-witness of marriage. Later, again, in 1979, there was granted to the episcopal conferences of Latin America the authority to install women in lay ministries, which they would choose to institute.[236] That fact alone answers the question of this section. May women be official lay ministers? Of course they may, because they are.

In 1973, long before the Latin American episcopal conferences sought and received permission to install women as non-ordained ministers, the Congregation for the Discipline of Sacraments had already issued the instruction, *Immensae Caritatis,* which instituted extraordinary ministers of the eucharist and prescribed that women as well as men might be installed in this ministry.[237] Non-ordained women ministers are a universal and well-established reality in the ministerial church today. That fact is plain to all who have eyes to see.

There is the possibility here for gross error. We can assume that the presence of women ministers in the church is a new fact of church life, a contemporary sop to obstreperous twentieth century women. And that assumption is quite false. Women ministers were part of the church's tradition from the beginning, and their reemergence today is just one more instance of the church attempting to recover the most ancient roots of its tradition. That historians of early Christianity have generally failed to notice the presence of women ministers is an oversight, I believe, that has two, not-unrelated roots. The first is the so-called chauvinism of the apostle Paul; the second the Mediterranean custom in which men were and are dominant and women were and are subject to them.

Twice in his first letter to the Corinthians, Paul makes statements on which the charge of chauvinism is always based. He writes: "I want you to understand that the head of every man is Christ, the head of woman is man, and the head of Christ is God" (11:3). Again: "Women should keep silent in the churches. For they are not permitted to speak, but should be subordinate, as even the law says" (14:34). At first sight it appears to be a pretty damning proscription of women, but only at first sight. Closer reading, not only of these texts but also of the entire Pauline corpus, indicates that Paul is not nearly as much a chauvinist as he has been accused of being.

The text in 14:34 can sustain no judgment against Paul, for it is "probably not written by Paul, but interpolated later," probably by the later and unknown writer of the first letter to Timothy, who makes the same statement in 2:11-14.[238] Paul, therefore, cannot be blamed for it. Besides, it contradicts what he had already clearly asserted in chapter 11. There, after the text cited above, he goes on to say that "any woman who prays or prophesies with her head unveiled dishonors her head—it is the same as if her head were shaven" (11:5).

What is remarkable in this text is not that Paul prescribes that a woman should be veiled in the church assembly, for that is a normal Jewish custom of the time.[239] No, what is remarkable is that he allows women to pray and prophesy in the assembly at all, for that was far from the custom. Indeed, it is probably because it was so far from the custom that Paul wants women "properly" veiled, to minimize the astonishment, confusion and, perhaps, indignation engendered by their praying and prophesying in public. This is not the behavior of a chauvinist, but of a man who takes seriously the equality in Christ he will later enunciate clearly in Gal. 3:28, with which I have already dealt. When we advert to the fact that, in the early church, prophets frequently led the community eucharist,[240] Paul's legitimation of women prophets in Corinth becomes even more suggestive.

But women prophets and prayers in Corinth is far from the whole story of women ministers in the missionary churches. Paul had a number of women colleagues in his ministry. There is Prisca with her husband Aquila, whom he greets in Rom.16:3 as *synergous,* fellow-workers, the very same word he uses to describe Timothy (Rom.16:21) and Apollos (1 Cor.3:9), as well as the lesser-known Epaphroditus (Phil.2:25) and Clement (Phil. 4:3). There is Phoebe, whom he commends as "a *diakonos* of the church at Cenchreae" (Rom 16:1). *Diakonos* is an ambiguous word in the New Testament, sometimes meaning an officially designated minister and sometimes meaning anyone who performs a service. But, in the case of Phoebe, the unexpected use of the male form *diakonos* rather than the female form is persuasive evidence that she is a designated minister.

Finally, there is Junia, whom Paul commends with Andronicus (probably her husband) as "outstanding among the apostles" (Rom.16:7).[241] *Apostle* is a momentous designation for Paul, and he devotes much energy to clarifying its meaning (Rom. 11:13; 1 Cor. 4:8-13; 9:1-7; 2 Cor. 12:11-12). It is unlikely that he would have assigned such an important word to a woman unless he considered it, in fact, true. Coworker, *diakonos*, apostle: were the women who bore these titles ordained? No, they were not. But, then, neither was anyone else ordained for ministry at this time, not even Peter or James or John or Paul or Apollos. But they were clearly non-ordained ministers as we have explained that title, Prisca and Phoebe and Junia every bit as much as Peter and Paul and Apollos.

Prisca, Phoebe and Junia were not the only women ministers in the early missionary churches. There were others,[242] but I do not see any need to deal with them too. For the fact of non-ordained women ministers is not established by numbers, but by one case alone. I have no doubt that ministers in the earliest New Testament churches were predominantly male. That is what one would expect, and that is what the evidence seems to support. But neither do I have any doubt that women ministers played significant leadership roles. That that situation had become culturally impossible in the patriarchal cultures represented in the Pastoral Epistles does not gainsay the fact that the church of Christ was originally a church of equal women and men ministers. It is precisely that situation of gender equality in Christ that the church, somewhat hesitantly, is beginning to validate again in our day.

A commentary on a comment will conclude this section. The comment was made by Cardinal Hume of Westminster on his return from the 1987 Synod. "Bishops," he said, "repeatedly called for the free and equal access of women to all aspects of the church's life which are not dependent on ordination."[243] Interestingly, essentially the same comment was made by Canadian Archbishop Hayes and American Archbishop Weakland.[244] After all I have said, commentary is easy.

In a church of equal disciples, there should be no institutionalized inferiority or discrimination. But as long as jurisdiction, in parishes, dioceses and in the universal church, is essentially linked to the power of orders, such discrimination will be inevitable. Jurisdiction will continue to be closed to lay women, and to lay men too, even when they are competent, as they were obviously competent for a Synod on the Laity.

To be an acolyte, a lector, a minister of baptism, of eucharist, of marriage, to be a non-ordained minister of any kind, is a gift of the Spirit. But until there are lay women and men, as well as clerics, dealing with the matters that affect decisions in a specific region or in the universal church, the unequal-disciples practice of the church will continue to be a tension-producing mismatch for its equal-disciples theory. Much has been achieved in the church in the name of equality and justice, but much also remains to be achieved. Until it is achieved, the Catholic Church cannot retrieve its rightful place in the vanguard of the struggle for the equal dignity and rights of lay women and of their lay brothers.

Women and Ordained Ministry

As the case of Phoebe clearly demonstrates, the designation *diakonos* was applied to women as well as men in the earliest church. Even the first letter of Timothy which, as we saw above, contains the most restrictive instructions for the conduct of women has a section which specifies the conduct required of deacons, women as well as men (3:8-13). There is no indication whatever in the text that the reference is to deacons' wives, as the most common interpretation would have us believe. The reference is clearly to women deacons. It is equally clear and not disputed that, by the third century, ordination of female deacons (deaconesses) was widespread in the eastern Catholic churches, though not in the west.[245]

There is no need for us to dwell, therefore, on the ordination of women to the ministry of the diaconate as if it were something entirely new in the People of God. It is not something new, but something to be renewed in the ancient tradition. The renewal would show that, in a church which is a community of equal disciples, talent/charism from the Spirit of God, not gender, is *the* criterion for ordination to diaconal ministry. As I testified earlier when dealing with the talent/charism required for ministry, there are many women who have been professionally interviewed and who have been found to match the talent/charism required for ordination to the diaconate. For such women to be again ordained requires only that the church renew its ancient tradition.

The real question of this section is the question of the ordination of women to the priesthood. Some may be surprised that the question is even raised, for they may assume that it was pre-empted by the publication in 1976 of *Inter Insigniores,* the Declaration on the Question of the Admission of Women to the Ministerial Priesthood.[246] But the case is far from closed. Noting that the Declaration was issued by the Congregation for the Doctrine of the Faith and not by the Pope *motu proprio,* Schillebeeckx points out that "this is the Roman way of keeping a matter open, though provisionally a kind of 'magisterial statement' on the issue has been made."[247]

Karl Rahner agrees that the question remains open. He emphasizes that the Declaration does not have the characteristics of a definitive, infallible teaching and, therefore, could be erroneous and reformable (which is not the same thing as saying that it *is*).[248] That being so, theologians are called upon to perform their normal ecclesial task of "interpreting the documents of the past and present magisterium, of putting them in the context of the whole of revealed truth, and of finding a better understanding of them by the use of hermeneutics."[249] However risky that task might be and is today, it is a task which must be done for the continued building up of the communion that is the Body of Christ.

A central point of the Declaration's "none too lucid argument"[250] is the transition it makes from the concept of the exclusively male apostles chosen by Jesus to the concept of the presbyter-bishop. In his *Christifideles Laici,* John Paul II makes the same transition without comment as if it were a well-known and agreed historical fact.[251] As is evident even from a cursory understanding of the historical development of those ministers, the transition is much too simplistic and far from a historical fact.[252] Rahner accuses it of ignoring "all the difficult questions about the concrete emergence of the church and its origin from Jesus, *even though they are of the greatest importance for its theme.*"[253] We know that it ignores specifically the women ministers we discovered in the New Testament churches, and very specifically Junia "outstanding among the apostles."

Scholars know full well that there are many cases in which the emerging church departed from the actions of Jesus. Seeking to situate the documents of the Magisterium in the context of the whole of revealed truth, and not just of recent Catholic history, the theologian is impelled to raise the question. If the emerging catholic church felt free to depart from well-remembered sayings and behaviors of Jesus in many other cases, how can the contemporary Roman Catholic Church not be equally free in the case of admitting women to its ordained priesthood? It is thoroughly specious to argue, ignoring the facts of Christian history, that "we cannot change what our Lord did or his call to women."[254]

Schillebeeckx calls attention to a kind of double hermeneutical standard applied to the actions of Jesus. Why, he asks, must the fact that Jesus chose only men as apostles have absolute and immutable theological significance, while the fact that he chose for the most part only married men is granted no significance whatever?[255] He could have appended a long list of similar questions about cases where the actions of the Roman church is at variance with the actions of Jesus.

Why, he might have asked, when there is a well-remembered saying of Jesus, "Whoever divorces his wife and marries another commits adultery" (Mark 10:11; cf. Matt. 5:32 and 19:9; Luke 16:18), did Paul feel free to make a quite different regulation (1 Cor. 7:15)? Why did the medieval church accept Paul's exception to Jesus' statement as the Pauline Privilege, create and approve its own exception in the distinction between *matrimonium ratum* and *matrimonium ratum et consummatum,* create and approve other exceptions in the so-called Petrine Privilege, all as ways to do what Jesus is remembered to have prohibited, namely, put asunder what God has joined (cf. Mark 10:9; Matt.19:6)? Why did the earliest Jewish-Christian church in Jerusalem, without any warrant from Jesus, make the extraordinary judgment that "you abstain from what has been sacrificed to idols and from blood and from what is strangled and from unchastity" (a judgment surely forgotten by those Christians who continue to eat *Blutwurst* or chicken)? Why, indeed, if not because "it has seemed good to the Holy Spirit and to us" (Acts 15:28).

The important teaching of the Second Vatican Council on the composition of the gospels, surprisingly, has something to teach us here. "The sacred authors wrote the four gospels," it teaches, "selecting some things from the many which had been handed on by word of mouth or in writing, reducing some of them to a synthesis, explicating some things *in view of the situation of their churches.*"[256] The gospels of Jesus, according to the prevailing Roman Catholic teaching, were adapted to respond to the needs of the churches at the time of their writing, not to record biographically everything that Jesus said and did. Under the guidance of the Holy Spirit, to whom John assigns "the double function of *recalling the original message of Jesus* and of *revealing new truth,* and thus of *re*proclaiming the truth of Jesus,[257] the kerygma proclaimed the meaning of the glorified Christ for the churches, not merely what the historical Jesus said and did. They told the honest truth about what Jesus said and did, but only in relation to the needs of the churches of the day.

The kerygma of Jesus was not the only thing adapted to respond to the needs of the churches. Their ministry was also adapted. How else could the monarchical episcopacy, found nowhere in the earliest churches, have come into existence and have become dominant? How else could the ministry of women, under only the restriction of custom and propriety that they be veiled, have vanished in the sub-apostolic church? History demonstrates that the church has always felt free to adapt to needs beyond the warrants directly derived from Jesus, and that both the apostolic and sub-apostolic churches used that freedom to the utmost. The rule that it can do only what Jesus did is a rule more broken by the church than observed. The argument based on it is a "none too lucid argument," reached on the basis of a selectively-forgetful hermeneutic. Such an argument can make no honest contribution to the modern discussion of the ordination of women to the hierarchical priesthood.

Another arm of the argument of the Declaration rests on the constant teaching of the church that the priest acts in the person of Christ. A common opinion is cited in Aquinas' formulation, "sacramental signs represent through a natural similarity."[258] It is used to sustain the argument that, unless the Priest who acts in the place of Christ is a man, it is difficult to perceive the image of Christ "who was and remains a man."[259]

It is one thing, though, as I argued previously, to state that a priest acts in the place of Christ, that he is a vicar of Christ, and quite another thing to ground and explain that assertion theologically. I have already suggested that the priest is a vicar of Christ, a representative of the glorified Christ, the only Christ there now is, only to the extent that he is first a vicar of the church, a representative of the mystical Christ. That argument needs to be extended and to be further reflected upon. I will extend it by connecting it with other aspects of revealed truth.

I begin in the foundational text, "Therefore a man leaves his father and his mother and cleaves to his wife, and they become one body" (Gen.2:24). This text founds the unity of a man and a woman in marriage in both Judaism and Christianity, the unity not only of their bodies in the act of sexual intercourse, but also of their entire persons. For, in the Hebrew culture from which the text emerges, *body* implies the entire person. "One personality would translate it better, for 'flesh' (body) in the Jewish idiom means 'real human life'."[260] In marriage, a man and a woman enter into such an intimate union that they become one life and one person. The ancient Rabbis teach that they become *'adam*, the full human being, and that it is only in the marital union that the image of God may be discerned in them.[261]

Aware of this long-established Jewish tradition, the unknown writer of the letter to the Ephesians can write that "husbands should love their wives as (for they are) their own bodies." Since this is so, and taken for granted to be so, he can state without any further explanation: "He who loves his wife loves himself" (5:28). He (or she?) cites Genesis 2:24 and then proceeds to something quite unexpected. "This mystery is a profound one and I am saying that it refers to Christ and the church" (5:32). The mystery, as the Anchor Bible seeks to show, is that Gen. 2:24 "has an eminent secret meaning," which is that it refers not just to a man and a woman in marriage but also to Christ and the church.

As a man and a woman become one person in the union of marriage, so also do Christ and the church become one person in their union. As wives may be described positively and without debasement as their husbands bodies, so also the church may be, and is extensively, described as the Body of Christ (1 Cor. 6:12-20; 10:17; 12:12-27; Rom. 12:4-5; Eph. 1:22-23; 2:14-16; 3:6; 4:4-16; 5:22-30; Col.1:18, 24; 2:19; 3:15). As in the ancient symbol a wife is not only her husband's body but also her husband, so also is the church not only the Body of Christ but also Christ.

Henri de Lubac has demonstrated beyond anyone's reasonable doubt that the understanding of the church as *the* body of Christ in human history continued for the first millenium of the church's existence.[262] During this time the church was known as the true body of Christ (*corpus Christi verum*), and valid ordination required that a man be appointed to a pastoral function in this body. Ordination without appointment to pastoral function in the church was called absolute ordination, and was proscribed by the Council of Chalcedon (451).[263] Precisely because he had a pastoral function of leadership in the true body of Christ, an ordained priest had also a function of leadership in the celebration of eucharist, the mystical body of Christ (*corpus Christi mysticum*).

For a millenium, then, the ordained priest celebrated the mystical Body of Christ for the true body of Christ only because and to the extent that he had also a pastoral function in that true body. In fact, he did not celebrate eucharist *for* the body but concelebrated it *with* the body. For we have Guerricus of Igny's report of the universal opinion that a priest "does not sacrifice by himself, he does not consecrate by himself, but the whole assembly of believers consecrates and sacrifices along with him."[264] In the celebration of the eucharist, the entire church, female and male believers alike, acted in the place of Christ because the entire church, female and male alike, *was* Christ according to the ancient symbolism. The ordained priest acted in the place of the church and, only because and to the extent that he was a designated represenative of the church, also in the person of Christ.

In the second millenium of the church's existence, the terms true Body of Christ (*corpus Christi verum*) and mystical Body of Christ (*corpus Christi mysticum*) became interchanged, the former now being applied to the eucharist and the latter to the church. Medieval theology responded to that change of perspective with a change of its own. It introduced a new distinction of power. To celebrate the true Body of Christ, the eucharist, a man needed the power of orders (*potestas ordinis*), which he received in ordination. To function pastorally in the mystical Body of Christ, the church composed of both females and males, he needed the power of jurisdiction (*potestas iurisdictionis*), which he received from a bishop after ordination.

These two changes in both theory and practice focused such exclusive attention on the eucharist as the true Body of Christ, and on the ordained priest as the one who had power over this true Body, that it became easy, indeed inevitable, for theology to focus the meaning of vicar of Christ exclusively on the ordained priest. But those changes in it can in no way gainsay the ancient tradition of a thousand years. The church, composed of those females and males who have put on Christ in baptism, whether it be named *corpus Christi verum* or *corpus Christi mysticum, is* Christ sacramentally every bit as much as the church's eucharist is.

If, within the context of the *entire* tradition of catholic truths, the priest is directly vicar of the church and only indirectly vicar of Christ, then the theological argument of the Declaration is unsound and, therefore, untenable. If the priest acts directly in the person of the ecclesial Body of Christ, and if that Body is composed of equal Christian males and females, then Aquinas' principle that "sacramental signs represent through a natural similarity" demands that the ordained priesthood should be composed of both males and females. That females as well as males would then indirectly represent Christ yields no insoluble problematic. For their putting on Christ and their incorporation into Christ in baptism not only already permits females to represent Christ, but also demands that they represent him. Their ordination into the order of priests would do no more than underscore that demand, just as it presently does for male priests.

One more step is required to complete my argument in this section. It is a step already found as early as the genuinely Pauline letters. It originates with a surprising question. Which Christ is it that both the church and the eucharist symbolize? It is a surprising question because the answer seems to be obvious; there is only one Christ. But, however true that assertion may be, it is not really an answer to the question posed. There is, indeed, only one Christ. But, after the resurrection, that Christ is not the baby Jesus of Bethlehem, or the child Jesus of the Temple, or the praying Jesus of Gethsemane, or the dying and dead Jesus of Calvary. The only Christ there is today is the Christ whom God raised from the dead. Though that Christ is in continuity with the baby Jesus and the dying Jesus, he is not identical with either. For he has been transformed.

When God raised Jesus of Nazareth from the dead, he transformed him. He transformed him totally, from dishonor to glory, from weakness to power, from physical body to spiritual body (cf. 1 Cor.15:35-45), so that if women or men in physical bodies were to see him, they would not recognize him (cf. Luke 24:13-31; John 20:11-17; 21:1-14). He transformed him into the new 'adam, "a life-giving spirit" (1 Cor.15:45), who leads to life for all men and women (eis pantas anthropous) (Rom. 5:18). This new 'adam sums up in himself all humankind, female as well as male, as did the old 'adam (Gen. 1:27; 5:2), only more abundantly (Rom. 5:15-17). It would seem that if ordained priests are to act as vicars of this Christ, the only one there now is, this would best be accomplished by a priesthood inclusive of both men and women.

The unsupported protestations of the Congregation for the Doctrine of the Faith notwithstanding,[265] Paul's original insight, noted several times already, still sums up this Christ best. "There is neither Jew nor Greek, there is neither slave nor free, there is neither male nor female, for you are all one person in Christ Jesus" (Gal. 3:28). For the first time since Paul gave voice to that insight, the western churches have the opportunity to incarnate it in their most solemn and formal activity, namely, the meal in which they keep memory of the Christ whom God raised raised from the dead.

I have sought to show that the Declaration's claim, that to act as vicar of Christ the priest must be a man, is inaccurate on two counts. First, it both misunderstands and misrepresents the nature of symbolism in general and the nature of the symbolism involved in the Bodies of Christ in particular. Secondly, it misunderstands the glorified nature of the Christ who is to be symbolized in the Bodies of Christ. I have sought, though, not simply to show that the Declaration is inaccurate but, employing the Declaration's own principles, also to advance ecclesial arguments for the ordination of women to the priesthood. While I know that there are questions other than theological with the ordination of women in the western churches, cultural, sociological and political questions, I have restricted myself only to theological arguments. For it is on those grounds that traditional arguments against ordination pretend to rest.

Summary

This chapter has been about women and ministry, founded in Pope John Paul II's judgment that "only through openly acknowledging the personal dignity of women is the first step taken to promote the full participation of women in church life."[266] It argued that women and men are equal disciples of Jesus and, therefore, equal in both Christian dignity and the Christian spirituality that is ministry; that both women and men have received from the Spirit of God the talent/charism for non-ordained ministry and that the church, both past and present, has recognized their charisms by installing them equally in such ministry; that the none too lucid arguments of the Declaration on the Question of the Admission of Women to the Ministerial Priesthood are unsound and untenable and, therefore, do not preempt discussion of the admission of women into the ordained order of priests.

In this chapter, I sought to offer ecclesial and sacramental arguments for the admission of equally Christian women to the ordained priesthood, though I would never pretend that such arguments are probatory beyond dispute. For, in a church in which all is mystery, nothing is open to apodictic, Euclidean proof. Joan Chittister asks whether the ordination of women is a question of theology or of authority. She answers her own question with the story of a bishop who, having claimed that he had "a grave theological problem with the question of the ordination of women," proceeded to assure his audience that "if the church gave permission for the ordination of women, I would ordain a woman immediately."[267] There seems to be here some confusion and admixture of theology and authority. This chapter sought to clarify that, at least, catholic theology which takes account of the whole of catholic truth not only does not *proscribe* the ordination of women, but even *prescribes* it.

Questions for Reflection

1. What implications do you see for Christian ministry in the biblical information about the equality of women and men in the Christian church?

2. Are you surprised by the fact that there were non-ordained women ministers in the earliest churches, even one whom Paul calls an apostle? Does it make any difference to anything?

3. How do you feel about the principle that the church can do in the twentieth century only what Jesus did in the first? How do you feel about the fact that the church itself has broken this principle as much as it has followed it?

4. The Roman Declaration on the Question of the Admission of Women to the Ministerial Priesthood was issued by the Roman Congregation for the Doctrine of the Faith, and not by a Pope.

Does this make any difference to you? Why do you think it makes a big difference to the church's theologians?

5. Would you personally be comfortable if the pastor of your parish were a woman? If yes, can you articulate why? If no, can you articulate why not? Do your reasons either way derive from theological grounds or from some other grounds?

Suggested Reading

Boff, Leonardo. *The Base Communities Reinvent the Church* (New York: Orbis, 1986).

Borresen, Kari E. *Subordination and Equivalence: The Nature and Role of Women in Augustine and Thomas Aquinas* (Washington: University Press of America, 1981).

Chittister, Joan. *Women, Ministry and Church* (New York: Paulist, 1983).

Fiorenza, Elizabeth Schussler. *In Memory of Her: A Feminist Reconstruction of Christian Origins* (New York: Crossroad, 1983).

Micks, Marianne H. and Price, Charles P. *Toward a New Theology of Ordination: Essays on the Ordination of Women* (Somerville, Mass.: Greeno, Hadden, 1976).

Tetlow, Elizabeth M. *Women and Ministry in the New Testament* (New York: Paulist, 1980).

Endnotes

Abbreviations

AAS = *Acta Apostolicae Sedis: Commentarium Officiale* (Roma: Typis Polyglottis Vaticanis)

CL = John Paul II, *Christifideles Laici,* Apostolic Exhortation on the Laity.

DS = *Enchiridion Symbolorum Definitionum et Declarationum de Rebus Fidei et Morum* ed. H.Denzinger et A.Schoenmetzer (Editio 33 emendata et aucta; Freiburg: Herder, 1965)

DV = *The Documents of Vatican II,* ed. Walter M. Abbott (London: Chapman, 1966)

MD = *La Maison Dieu* (Paris: Editions du Cerf)

PG = *Patrologiae Cursus Completus: Series Graeca,* ed. J.P.Migne

PL = *Patrologiae Cursus Completus: Series Latina,* ed. J.P. Migne

SC = *Sacrorum Conciliorum Nova et Amplissima Collectio,* ed. J.D. Mansi (Paris: Hubert Welter, 1903-1927)

TS = *Theological Studies* (Georgetown University)

All abbreviations in the Endnotes are listed without any underlined emphasis. All translations from languages other than English are the author's.

Notes

1. See CL, n. 2.

2. Pastoral Constitution on the Church in the Modern World, n. 62, DV 270.

3. International Theological Commission, *Theses on the Relationship Between the Ecclesiastical Magisterium and Theology* (Washington: United States Catholic Conference, 1977), 6.

4. *Comment. in Rom.*, Cap. 1, Lectio VI, in *Opera Omnia* (New York: Misurgia Publishers, 1949), Vol. XIII, 15. See also, George Klubertanz, *St. Thomas Aquinas on Analogy: A Textual Analysis and Systematic Synthesis* (Chicago: Loyola University Press, 1960).

5. See his Apostolic Letter "On the Dignity and Vocation of Women," n. 8.

6. See "The Unknown God," in *The von Balthasar Reader*, ed. M. Kehl and Werner Loser (New York: Crossroad, 1982), 181-187.

7. See John Paul II, "On the Dignity and Vocation of Women," n. 6 and 8.

8. For a more extended version of this discussion, see Michael G. Lawler, *Raid on the Inarticulate: An Invitation to Adult Religion* (Washington: University Press of America, 1980), esp. 45-68.

9. See The Final Report, "The Church, in the Word of God, Celebrates the Mysteries of Christ for the Salvation of the World" (National Catholic News Service), II,C,1; also CL, n. 19.

10. AAS 55 (1963): 848.

11. Reported in *The Tablet*, November 7, 1987, 1203.

12. Edward Schillebeeckx, *L'Eglise du Christ et l'homme d'aujourd'hui selon Vatican II* (Paris: Mappus, 1965).

13. Edward Schillebeeckx, *Jesus: An Experiment in Christology*, trans. Hubert Hoskins (New York: Seabury, 1979), 438.

14. CL, n. 19.

15. Constitution on the Church, n. 1, DV 14.

16. Cf. Didymus, *In Psalmos*, 71,5, PG 39, 1465.

17. Cf. Augustine, *In Joannis Evangelium Tractatus VI*, c.1, n. 7, PL 35, 1428.

18. Constitution on the Sacred Liturgy, n.7, DV 140-141.

19. Constitution on the Church, n.4, DV 16.

20. Cf. *Théophile d'Antioche: Trois Livres à Autolychus*, trans, J. Sender (Paris: Cerf, 1948), 1, 12, 85; Rufinus, *Comment.in Symb.Apost.*, PL 21, 345; Augustine, *De Vita Christiana*, PL 40, 1033, and *Enarr. in Ps. XXVI*, PL 36, 200; Jerome, *Comment.in Ps 104*, in *Corpus Christianorum, Series Latina*, LXXII, 230, and *Tract. de Ps. 104*, ibid., LXXVIII.

21. Constitution on the Church, n. 12, DV 30; CL, n. 24.

22. *Constitutiones Apostolicae*, II, 26, PG 1, 667.

23. Constitution on the Church, n. 1, DV 15.

24. Ibid., n. 9, DV 26.

25. DS 1639.

26. See K. Rahner and H. Vorgrimler, "Grace," in *Concise Theological Dictionary* (London: Burns and Oates, 1965), 194.

27. Cf. Michael G. Lawler, *Symbol and Sacrament: A Contemporary Sacramental Theology* (New York: Paulist, 1988).

28. Constitution on the Church, n. 4, DV 17.

29. Constitution on the Church, n. 33, DV 59; CL, n. 14.

30. See Yves Congar, "L'ecclesia ou communauté chrétienne sujet intégrale de l'action liturgique," in *La Liturgie d'après Vatican II* (Paris, 1967), 241-282; B. Botte, "Note historique sur la concélébration dans l'église ancienne," MD 35 (1953): 9-23; R. Raes, "La concélébration dans les rites orientaux," ibid., 24-47.

31. Constitution on the Church, n. 26, DV 50.

32. *I Remember* (New York: Crossroad, 1985), 96.

33. AAS 59 (1967): 1044.

34. N.33, DV 60.

35. Roma: Gregorian University Press, 1937.

36. See the remarks of Cardinal Liénart, *Acta Concilii Vaticani Secundi*, I, 4, 126-127.

37. Constitution on the Church, n.8, DV 23.

38. Ibid., n. 48, DV 78.

39. Decree on Ecumenism, n.6, DV 350.

40. Constitution on the Church, n. 48, DV 79.

41. Cf. Ibid.

42. Ibid., n. 5, DV 18.

43. See Paul Minear, *Images of the Church in the New Testament* (Philadelphia: Westminster, 1960) and Yves Congar, *L'Eglise de Saint Augustin à l'époque moderne* (Paris: Cerf, 1970).

44. New York: Doubleday, 1974.

45. *Models of the Church*, 9.

46. "The Church, in the Word of God, Celebrates the Mysteries of Christ for the Salvation of the World," II,C,1.

47. Constitution on the Church, n.9, DV 25.

48. *Redemptor Hominis*, n.21, AAS 71 (1979): 317.

49. See "Propositions on the Doctrine of Christian Marriage," in *Origins*, September 28, 1978, 237.

50. CL, n.57.

51. DS 1532. See Lawler, *Symbol and Sacrament*, 36-45.

52. *The Code of Canon Law* (London: Collins, 1983), Can.205. My emphasis.

53. Constitution on the Sacred Liturgy, n.59, DV 158.

54. See above, note 1.

55. *Jesus: The Death and Resurrection of God* (Atlanta: John Knox, 1985).

56. *L'Evangile et l'Eglise* (Paris, 1902), 111.

57. See Arnold Van Gennep, *The Rites of Passage* (London: Routledge and Kegan Paul, 1960).

58. *Catechesis XX, Mystagogica III*, PG 33, 1079.

59. *De Zelo et Livore*, 12, PL 4, 646.

60. *De Bono Patientiae*, 9, PL 4, 628.

61. CL, n. 32.

62. Constitution on the Church, n. 1, DV 15.

63. See Lawler, *Symbol and Sacrament*.

64. *Ad Philadelph.*, 4, in *The Fathers of the Church*, Vol.1 (Washington: Catholic University of America Press, 1962), 114.

65. Dom Gregory Dix, *The Shape of the Liturgy* (London: Dacre Press, 1945) 21.

66. See Patrick McCaslin and Michael G. Lawler, *Sacrament of Service: A Vision of the Permanent Diaconate Today* (New York: Paulist, 1986) and John F. Booty, *The Servant Church: Diaconal Ministry and the Episcopal Church* (Wilton, CT: Morehouse-Barlow, 1982).

67. DS 1776.

68. Constitution on the Church, n. 28, DV 53.

69. See *Origins*, November 5, 1987, 380.

70. Cf. Thomas F. O'Meara, *Theology of Ministry* (New York: Paulist, 1983), 136.

71. See CL, n. 21-22.

72. Ernst Käsemann, "Ministry and Community in the New Testament," in *Essays on New Testament Themes*, trans. W.J. Montague (Naperville, Illinois: Allenson, 1964), 74.

73. CL, n. 24.

74. See Edward Schillebeeckx, *Ministry: Leadership in the Community of Jesus Christ* (New York: Crossroad, 1981), 24.

75. CL, n. 24.

76. Constitution on the Church, n. 12, DV 30.

77. Lawler, *Symbol and Sacrament*, 51.

78. Constitution on the Church, n. 31, DV 57.

79. See his *Lay People in the Church: A Study For A Theology of Laity* (Westminster: Newman Press, 1959), 1-21.

80. James D.G. Dunn, *Unity and Diversity in the New Testament* (Philadelphia: Westminster, 1977), p. 114.

81. C. Spicq, *Les Epîtres Pastorales*, I (Paris: Gabalda, 1969) 73. See also J. Crowe, *The Acts* (Wilmington: Glazier, 1979), 156; E. Schillebeeckx, *Ministry: Leadership in the Community of Jesus Christ*, 18 and 146.

82. See Spicq, *Les Epîtres Pastorales*, 71.

83. See *Epist. ad Magnesios*, 2, PG 5, 758; *Epist. ad Smyrneos*, 8-9, PG 5, 714; *Epist. ad Polycarpum*, PG 5, 718.

84. *Epist. ad Smyrneos*, 8, PG 5, 714.

85. *Epist. ad Ephes.*, 4, PG 5, 714.

86. See Raymond Brown, *Priest and Bishop: Biblical Reflections* (New York: Paulist, 1970), 40-43.

87. *Adv.Haereses*, IV, 26, 3-4, PG 7, 1053.

88. Ibid. III, 3, PG 7, 848-854.

89. Cf. David Power, *Ministers of Christ and His Church* (London: Chapman, 1969), 45.

90. *Epist. LXV*, 3, PL 4, 396.

91. *Epist. LXIX*, 8, PL 4, 406.

92. *Epist. XXVII*, 1, PL 4, 298.

93. *Epist. LXVII*, 4-5, in *Saint Cyprien: Correspondence*, ed. Louis Bayard (Paris: Belles Lettres, 1925), 229-231; see also P. Granfield, "Episcopal Election in Cyprian: Clerical and Lay Participation," *TS* 37 (1976): 41-52.

94. *Epist. LIX*, 5, PL 4, 336.

95. *Epist. LXVI*, 1, PL 4, 398; also *Epist. LXVII*, 1, in *Saint Cyprien*, 228.

96. *Epist. I*, 1, in *Saint Cyprien*, 2.

97. *Epist. LXI*, 3, in ibid., 195.

98. *Epist. XII*, 1, in ibid., 33; *Epist. V*, 2, in ibid., 13.

99. *Epist. XVIII*, 2, in ibid., 51.

100. There is an earlier use of the word *laikos* in Clement of Rome's Letter to the Corinthians. But it is not clear that the word has the connotation which will be given it later by Clement of Alexandria and succeeding generations. See Alexandre Faivre, "The Laity in the First Centuries: Issues Revealed by Historical Research," in *Lumen Vitae* XLII (1987): 132.

101. *Stromatum*, III, 12, PG 8, 1191.

102. *De Exhortatione Castitatis*, VII, PL 2, 922.

103. *Comment. in Isaiam Prophetam*, Lib. V, Cap. 19, PL 24, 185.

104. See Nathan Mitchell, *Mission and Ministry: History and Theology of the Sacrament of Order* (Wilmington: Glazier, 1982), 207-215; also Pierre Van Beneden, *Aux origines d'une terminologie sacramentelle: ordo, ordinare, ordinatio* (Louvain: Spicilegium Sacrum Lovaniense, 1974).

105. *Epist. II*, 3, 5, PL 20, 472.

106. *Epist. XIV*, 4, PL 54, 672-673.

107. *Decretum*, II, Causa XII, Q.1, c.7.

108. See Henri de Lubac, *Corpus Mysticum: l'eucharistie et l'église au Moyen Age*, 2nd.ed. (Paris: Aubier, 1949).

109. SC 22, 982.

110. See *Vita Zephyrini*, ed. L. Duchesne, I:139, cited in E. Schillebeeckx, *Ministry*, 152, note 44.

111. *De Purificatione B. Mariae Sermo* 5, PL 185, 87.

112. "L'ecclesia ou communauté chrétienne, sujet intégrale de l'action liturgique," in *La Liturgie d'après Vatican II* (Paris, 1967), 241-282; see also B. Botte, "Note historique sur la concélébration dans l'église ancienne," MD 35 (1953): 9-23; R. Raes, "La concélébration eucharistique dans les rites orientaux," in ibid., 24-47.

113. Constitution on the Church, n.30, DV 57.

114. CL, n. 9.

115. Can. 204,1.

116. Can. 207,1.

117. Can.208.

118. AAS 64 (1972):208.

119. CL, n.15.

120. Can.225,2.

121. See, for instance, CL, n.4; also his Address to the Bishops of Switzerland and his Address to the Priests of Switzerland, AAS 71 (1985): 56, 64, 67.

122. CL, n.2.

123. The Ministry and Life of Priests, n.9, DV 552.

124. Robert Kinast, "Laity View Their Roles in Church and World," in *Origins*, Vol. 17, n.16, 95-99.

125. Ibid., p.96.

126. Constitution on the Church, n.8, DV 24.

127. John A.T. Robinson, "Christianity's 'No' to Priesthood," in *The Christian Priesthood* ed. N. Lash and J. Rhymer (London: Darton, Longman, Todd, 1970), 4. See also Raymond E. Brown, *Priest and Bishop: Biblical Reflections* (London: Chapman, 1971; James P. Mackey, *Modern Theology: A Sense of Direction* (New York: Oxford University Press, 1987), 142-143; Kenan B. Osborne, *Priesthood: A History of the Ordained Ministry in the Roman Catholic Church* (New York: Paulist Press, 1988), 40-85; E. Schillebeeckx, *Ministry: A Case for Change* (New York: Crossroad, 1981).

128. Robinson, "Christianity's 'No'," 4.

129. George Tavard, *A Theology for Ministry* (Wilmington: Glazier, 1983), 120.

130. John H. Elliott, *The Elect and the Holy* (Leiden: Brill, 1966), 28.

131. See ibid., passim; Schillebeeckx, *Ministry*, 51.

132. *De purificatione B. Mariae Sermo*, PL 185, 87.

133. *Constitutiones Apostolicae* III, 15, PG 1, 798.

134. *Théophile d'Antioche: Trois Livres à Autolychus*, trans. J. Sender (Paris: Cerf, 1948), 1, 12, 85. Cf. Rufinus, *Comment.in Symb. Apostolorum*, PL 21, 345.

135. *De Vita Christiana*, PL 40, 1033. Cf. *Enarratio in Ps. XXVI*, PL 36, 200.

136. Cited in J. Lecuyer, *Le Sacerdoce dans le Mystère du Christ* (Paris: Cerf, 1957), 201, n.1.

137. *Comment. in Ps. 104*, in *Corpus Christianorum, Series Latina* LXXII, 230; *Tract. de Ps. 104*, Ibid., LXXVIII, 190.

138. IIa-IIae, 85, 4. Cf. ibid., a.2.

139. Cf. Henri de Lubac, *Corpus Mysticum*.

140. Cf. Constitution on the Church, nn. 1, 9, 48, DV 15, 26, 79; Constitution on the Sacred Liturgy, nn. 5, 26, DV 140, 147; Decree on the Missionary Activity of the Church, n. 5, DV 589.

141. Cf. Schillebeeckx, *Ministry*, 29-30.

142. CL., n.14.

143. Ibid.

144. See Kenan B. Osborne, *Priesthood*, 89-129.

145. Cf. Raymond E. Brown, *Priest and Bishop*, 17-19.

146. See Jean Paul Audet, *La Didachè: Instruction des Apôtres* (Paris: Gabalda, 1958), 372-433.

147. See Francis Clark, *Eucharistic Sacrifice and the Reformation* (London: Darton, Longman and Todd, 1960).

148. Constitution on the Church, n.10, DV 27.

149. CL, n.22.

150. Ibid. cf. Pius XII, Allocutio *Magnificate Dominum*, in AAS, 46 (1954): 669.

151. B. Botte, *Hippolyte de Rome: La Tradition Apostolique* (Paris: Cerf, 1968), c.10, 67.

152. *The Minister of God: Effective and Fulfilled* (New York: Alba House, 1986), 38.

153. *A Letter on Priestly Formation*, October 1, 1979, 12.

154. *Ministry: A Theological, Pastoral Handbook* (San Francisco: Harper and Row, 1987), 51-71.

155. Those seeking more detail can consult McCaslin and Lawler, *Sacrament of Service*, 49-51.

156. Helen Doohan, *The Minister of God*, 18.

157. CL, n.14 and n.23.

158. Ibid., n.23.

159. Cf. David N. Power, *Gifts That Differ: Lay Ministries Established and Unestablished* (New York: Pueblo Publishing, 1980), 126-127.

160. Henri J.M. Nouwen, *Creative Ministry* (New York: Doubleday, 1971), 110.

161. See Lawler, *Symbol and Sacrament*, 126-153.

162. DS 1763. My emphasis.

163. DS 1770. My emphasis.

164. See *Concilium Tridentinum Diariorum, Actorum, Epistolarum, Tractatuum*, ed. Societas Goeresiana (Freiburg: Herder, 1901-1961), 9, 83.

165. DS 1771.

166. See, for example, A. Rohrbasser (ed.), *Sacerdotis Imago: Päpstliche Dokumente über des Priestertum von Pius X bis Joannes XXIII*, (Fribourg, 1962).

167. Alexandre Ganoczy, "'Splendors and Miseries' of the Tridentine Doctrine of Ministries," in *Concilium*, Vol. 10, n.8 (1972): 75.

168. See A. Dulles, *Models of the Church*.

169. See *Concilium Tridentinum* 5, 105-108.

170. Constitution on the Church, n. 25, DV 47.

171. Ibid., n. 28, DV 53.

172. Decree on the Life and the Ministry of Priests, n. 4, DV 538.

173. See ibid., nn. 2 and 5, DV 533-536 and 542-543; see also Constitution on the Church, nn. 26 and 28, DV 50 and 53.

174. See "Ratio Fundamentalis Institutionis Sacerdotalis," in AAS 62 (1970): 321-384, esp. 327-331.

175. See the publication of the French Bishops, *Tous Responsables dans l'Eglise?*, note 60.

176. Decree on the Ministry and Life of Priests, n.2, DV 534.

177. Ibid., n. 6, DV 545. See also "Ratio Fundamentalis," in AAS, 62 (1970): 329-330.

178. "Ratio Fundamentalis," in *AAS* 62 (1970): 330.

179. Decree on the Ministry and Life of Priests, n.4, DV 538.

180. Ibid., n.18, DV 569.

181. "Ratio Fundamentalis," 330.

182. "Ratio Fundamentalis," 357.

183. Decree on the Bishops' Pastoral Office, n.12, DV 404-405.

184. Decree on the Ministry and Life of Priests, n.6, DV 545.

185. Constitution on the Sacred Liturgy, n.10, DV 142; Decree on the Ministry and Life of Priests, n.5, DV 541.

186. The Ministry and Life of Priests, n.1, DV 533.

187. See J.P. Audet, "Literary Forms and Contents of a Normal *Eucharistia* in the First Century," in *Studia Evangelica: Papers Presented to the International Congress on the Four Gospels in 1957* (Berlin, 1959), 643-644.

188. *Sermo 340*, 1, PL 38, 1483.

189. The Ministry and Life of Priests, n.9, DV 552.

190. Ibid.

191. CL, n.14.

192. *Called and Gifted: Reflections of the American Bishops Commemorating the Fifteenth Anniversary of the Issuance of the Decree on the Apostolate of the Laity*, (Washington: NCCB, 1980).

193. See Lawler, *Symbol and Sacrament*, 29-34.

194. *Adv. Valentinianos*, 16, PL 2, 569; *De Praescript. Adv. Haeret.* 13, PL 2,26; Ibid., 28, PL 2, 40; *De Virginibus Velandis*, 1, PL 2, 889.

195. *Epist. 63*, 14, in *Saint Cyprien: Correspondence*, ed. Louis Bayard (Paris: Belles Lettres, 1925), 209; cf. *Epist. 59*, 5, ibid., 174. For the contributions of both Tertullian and Cyprian, see Michele Maccarone, *Vicarius Christi: Storia del Titolo Papale* (Roma: Lateranum, 1952), 26-35.

196. See Edward J. Kilmartin, "Apostolic Office: Sacrament of Christ," TS 36 (1975): 246.

197. Pius XII, *Mediator Dei*, AAS 39 (1947): 538-539, 553-556; *Mystici Corporis*, AAS 35 (1943): 232-233; Paul VI, *Mysterium Fidei*, AAS 57 (1965): 761-763.

198. Constitution on the Church, n.10, DV 27; cf. nn. 21, 28, 37, DV 40-41, 53-54, 64-65; The Ministry and the Life of Priests, nn. 2 and 13, DV 533-536 and 559-562.

199. "Apostolic Office: Sacrament of Christ," TS 36 (1975): 225.

200. Constitution on the Sacred Liturgy, n.7, DV 141.

201. See his Preface to Bernard D. Marliangeas, *Clés Pour Une Théologie du Ministère: In Persona Christi, In Persona Ecclesiae* (Paris: Beauchesne, 1978), 6. The entire work should be consulted for the question here under discussion, namely, *vicarius Christi-vicarius ecclesiae*.

202. See Michael G. Lawler, *Secular Marriage, Christian Sacrament* (Mystic: Twenty-Third Publications, 1985).

203. Botte, *La Tradition Apostolique*, 45 and 57.

204. Marliangeas, *Clés Pour Une Théologie du Ministère*, 14.

205. Apostolic Constitution *Pontificalis Romani*, AAS 60 (1968):373.

206. See Edward J. Kilmartin, "Ministère et ordination dans l'église chrétienne primitive," MD 138 (1979): 49-92.

207. Schillebeeckx, *Ministry*, 30.

208. Cf. *Ratio Fundamentalis*, AAS 62 (1970): 329. "Every priest is taken from the people of God and constituted for this same people. But although priests, in virtue of the sacrament of orders, carry out the task of both father and teacher, nevertheless with all the Christian faithful, they are disciples of the Lord . . . . They are brothers among brothers, as members of one and the same body of Christ." See also Yves Congar, "Ministères et structuration de l'église," MD 102 (1970): 7-20, and "La hierarchie comme service selon le Nouveau Testament et les documents de la tradition," in *L'épiscopat et l'église universelle* (Paris: Cerf, 1962), 67-100.

209. Cf. Constitution on the Church, nn. 39-42, DV 65-72; also CL, n.16-17.

210. Mitchell, *Mission and Ministry*, 302.

211. See Constitution on the Church, n.10, DV 27; Decree on the Apostolate of the Laity, n.2-3, DV 491- 492; also CL, n.9,14,15.

212. "Declaration on the Question of the Admission of Women to the Ministerial Priesthood," AAS 69 (1977): 98-116; CL, n. 49-51.

213. See John H. Martin, "The Injustice of Not Ordaining Women: A Problem for Medieval Theologians," TS 48 (1987): 303-316, and *Women Priests: A Catholic Commentary on the Vatican Declaration* eds. Leonard Swidler and Arlene Swidler (New York: Paulist, 1977).

214. n.9, DV 500.

215. II,C,6.

216. Reported in *Origins*, November 12, 1987, 387-389.

217. Joan Chittister, *Women, Ministry and the Church* (New York: Paulist, 1983), 1.

218. Reported in *The Tablet*, 7 November 1987, 127.

219. See CL, n.22-23.

220. See above, note 213; also CL, n.49.

221. *Pastoral Statement for Catholics on Biblical Fundamentalism* (Washington: United States Catholic Conference, March 26, 1987).

222. Dogmatic Constitution on Divine Revelation, n.12, DV 120. See also n.19, DV 124.

223. James D.G. Dunn, *Unity and Diversity in the New Testament*, 77.

224. See, e.g., Thomas Aquinas, *Summ. Theol.*, 1,92,1.

225. Partners in the Mystery of Redemption: A Pastoral Response to Women's Concerns for Church and Society, *Origins*, April 21, 1988, 762.

226. Elisabeth Schussler Fiorenza, "The Biblical Roots for the Discipleship of Equals," *The Journal of Pastoral Counseling* 14 (1979): 12.

227. Elisabeth Schussler Fiorenza, *In Memory of Her: A Feminist Theological Reconstruction of Christian Origins* (New York: Crossroad, 1983), 235. To understand the conclusion, one needs to read the entire section 205-236.

228. See Lawler, *Secular Marriage, Christian Sacrament*, 11-16.

229. Krister Stendahl, *The Bible and the Role of Women* (Philadelphia: Fortress, 1966), 37.

230. See AAS 64 (1972): 529-534 and 534-540.

231. AAS 64: 530. See Constitution on the Sacred Liturgy, n.14, DV 144.

232. *Gifts That Differ*, 31.

233. AAS 64: 531.

234. AAS 68 (1976): 62.

235. See "Brasilia: Relatorio sobre os Ministerios Liturgicos Exercidos por Leigos," *Notitiae* 11 (1975): 263-268.

236. Cited in Power, *Ministries That Differ*, note 38, 34.

237. AAS 65 (1973): 264-271.

238. See Reginald H. Fuller, "Pro and Con: the Ordination of Women in the New Testament," in Marianne H. Micks and Charles P. Price (eds.) *Toward a New Theology of Ordination: Essays on the Ordination of Women* (Somerville, MA: Greeno, Hadden, 1976), 6 and 9. The non-Pauline authorship of First Timothy is now so well established that I feel no need to demonstrate it here. Those who need information can consult any introduction to the New Testament.

239. See H.J. Schoeps, *Paul: The Theology of the Apostle in the Light of Jewish Religious History*, trans. H.Knight (Philadelphia: Westminster, 1961), 39.

240. See 1 Cor. 14:16 and J.P. Audet, *La Didachè*. The *Didachè* prescribes that prophets are to be allowed to preside at eucharist (10:7) and describes them as "High Priests" (13:13).

241. RSV, ignoring the obvious syntax, gratuitously and misleadingly renders *episemoi en tois apostolois*, "outstanding among the apostles," as "*men* of note among the apostles." Cranfield comments: "That the fourth Greek word of the verse should be accentuated as the accusative of the common Roman female name Junia is hardly to be doubted. The persistence of the accentuation which makes it the accusative of an hypothetical masculine name Junias seems to rest on nothing more solid than conventional prejudice." See C.E.B. Cranfield, *Romans: A Shorter Commentary* (Grand Rapids: Eerdmans, 1985), 377. See also M.J. Lagrange, *Saint Paul: Epître aux Romains*, (Paris: Gabalda, 1950), 366.

242. See Fiorenza, *In Memory of Her*, 160-199; Fuller, "Pro and Con," 1-10; Mary Evans, *Women in the Bible* (Exeter: Paternoster Press, 1983), 123-130; Manuel Miguens, *Church Ministries in New Testament Times* (Arlington: Christian Culture Press, 1976), 137-140; Leonard Swidler, *Biblical Affirmations of Woman* (Philadelphia: Westminster, 1979), 294-299; Rosemary Radford Reuther (ed.) *Religion in Sexism* (New York: Simon and Schuster, 1974), 117-147.

243. Reported in *The Tablet*, 7 November, 1987, 1225.

244. Reported in *Origins*, October 22, 1987, 343-345.

245. See Herbert Frohnhofen, "Weibliche Diakone in der frühen Kirche," in *Stimmen der Zeit* 111 (1986): 269- 278.

246. AAS 69 (1977): 98-116.

247. Schillebeeckx, *Ministry*, 96.

248. "Women and the Priesthood," in *Concern for the Church* (New York: Crossroad, 1981), 35-47.

249. International Theological Commission, *Theses on the Relationship Between the Ecclesiastical Magisterium and Theology* (Washington: United States Catholic Conference, 1977), 6.

250. Rahner, "Women and the Priesthood," 36.

251. See CL, n. 22; cf. CL, n.51.

252. See Mackey, *Modern Theology*, 125-156.

253. Rahner, "Women and the Priesthood," 40. My emphasis.

254. CL, n.51.

255. *Ministry*, 97.

256. Constitution on Divine Revelation, n.19, DV 124. My emphasis. The identical teaching is contained in the Pontifical Biblical Commission's "Instruction on the Historical Truth of the Gospels." See Joseph Fitzmyer's commentary on this instruction in TS 25 (1964): 386-408.

257. James Dunn, *Unity and Diversity in the New Testament*, 78.

258. In IV Sent., d.25, q.2, a.2, quaestiuncula 1, ad 4.

259. AAS 69 (1977): 110.

260. F.R. Barry, *A Philosophy from Prison* (London: SCM, 1926), 151. cf. E. Schillebeeckx, *Marriage: Secular Reality and Saving Mystery*, Vol. 1 (London: Sheed and Ward, 1965), 43; Markus Barth, *Ephesians: Translations and Commentary on Chapters Four to Six* (New York: Doubleday, 1974), 734-738; X. Léon-Dufour (ed.), *Vocabulaire de Théologie Biblique*, 2nd ed. rev. (Paris: Cerf, 1970), 146-152.

261. See Richard Batey, "The *mia sarx* union of Christ and the Church," *New Testament Studies* 13 (1966-67): 272.

262. See *Corpus Mysticum*, passim.

263. See J.D. Mansi (ed.), *Sacrorum Conciliorum Nova et Amplissima Collectio* (Paris: Welter, 1903-1927), Vol. 7, 394-395. See also Cyrille Vogel, "Titre d'ordination et lien du presbytre à la communauté locale dans l'église ancienne," in MD 115 (1973): 70-85, and "Vacua Manus Impositio: l'inconsistence de la chirotonie en Occident," in Mélanges Liturgiques offerts à Dom B. Botte (Louvain, 1972), 511-524.

264. *De Purificatione B. Mariae Sermo* 5, PL 185, 87. See also Yves Congar, "L'ecclesia ou communauté chrétienne sujet intégrale de l'action liturgique," in *La Liturgie d'après Vatican II* (Paris, 1967), 241-282, and B. Botte, "Note Historique sur la concélébration dans l'église ancienne," in MD 35 (1953): 9-23.

265. AAS 69 (1977): 110.

266. CL, n.49.

267. *Winds of Change: Women Challenge the Church* (Kansas City: Sheed and Ward, 1986), 84.